my Redeemer Lives!

Brigham Young University
Easter Conference

EDITED BY

RICHARD NEITZEL HOLZAPFEL AND KENT P. JACKSON

RSC
BYU

DESERET
BOOK

Published by the Religious Studies Center, Brigham Young University, Provo, Utah, in cooperation with Deseret Book Company, Salt Lake City
http://rsc.byu.edu

ISBN 978-0-8425-2784-2
Retail US $14.99

Cover painting: *Mary and the Resurrected Lord*, by Harry Anderson, © 2002 by Intellectual Reserve, Inc. All rights reserved.
Layout and design by Jeff Wade

Library of Congress Cataloging-in-Publication Data

BYU Easter Conference (2010 : Brigham Young University) My Redeemer lives!: Brigham Young University Easter Conference / edited by Richard Neitzel Holzapfel and Kent P. Jackson.

    p. cm.
  Includes bibliographical references and index.
    ISBN 978-0-8425-2784-2 (hardbound : alk. paper) 1. Jesus Christ—Passion—Congresses. 2. Jesus Christ—Resurrection—Congresses. 3. Easter—Congresses. I. Holzapfel, Richard Neitzel, 1954- editor. II. Jackson, Kent P. editor. III. Title.

BX8643.J4B97 2010
232—dc22

2010053562

CONTENTS

A flash of fire is seen inside the tomb, and the patriarch emerges. From his burning candles, the Holy Fire spreads rapidly to candles in the hands of thousands of worshipp ers. Thus the fire that comes from the place of Jesus' triumph over darkness spreads light all over the world.

(Courtesy of Kent P. Jackson.)

Introduction: Holy Fire

THROUGH DIFFERENT OBSERVANCES and ceremonies, Christians around the world express their faith that their Redeemer lives. Such beliefs are seen vividly in the Holy Land, where Christians of many varieties live and where many more come as pilgrims to visit locations where the sacred events of Jesus' life took place.

One of the most remarkable and memorable Easter observances is the celebration of the "Miracle of the Holy Fire," which takes place in Jerusalem on Holy Saturday, the day before Easter in the Orthodox Christian calendar. This extraordinary celebration of the Resurrection is observed in Eastern (Orthodox) Christianity but not in Western (Catholic/Protestant) churches. It has been documented for well over a thousand years. It is a unique practice in the world—it takes place only in the Holy City, yet it is loved throughout all of

Eastern Christianity and is even broadcast live in some Orthodox countries.

The Greek Orthodox patriarch presides over the ceremony, assisted by bishops of the Armenian and Syriac Orthodox Churches and others. The setting is the Church of the Resurrection, known to Western Christians as the Church of the Holy Sepulchre, the traditional site of Jesus' crucifixion, burial, and resurrection. Inside the church, the patriarch enters alone into the small, dark structure identified as the tomb of Jesus. Multitudes who have crowded inside the church wait, holding unlit candles in their hands. Eventually, a flash of fire is seen inside the tomb, and within a moment, the patriarch emerges, holding a bundle of burning candles.

From his burning candles, the Holy Fire spreads rapidly to candles in the hands of thousands of worshippers inside the great church. From there, the flame spreads outside the building to thousands more along the streets of Jerusalem's Old City. And then the flame is transported to distant lands as the celebration continues well beyond Jesus' tomb. Thus the fire that comes from the place of Jesus' triumph over darkness spreads light all over the world.

Throughout the year, our thoughts are directed toward our Savior. He is "the light of the world." Those who follow him "shall not walk in darkness, but shall have the light of life" (John 8:12). Like the flame that emerges from the empty tomb, Jesus emerged on that Easter morning to bring light to all people in all nations. We rejoice in that light.

The essays published in this book were delivered at annual Brigham Young University Easter Conferences in 2010 and 2011. We thank those who accepted our invitations to share their feelings, insights, and testimonies about the life and ministry of Jesus Christ. We hope that this small volume will add to your testimony that our Redeemer lives and that his saving light continues to illuminate our lives.

Richard Neitzel Holzapfel
Birmingham, Alabama

Kent P. Jackson
Jerusalem

Jesus Christ is our ever-present Friend. He is aware of falling sparrows and failing individuals. He controls the universe and everything in it. The ways He can help us are as innumerable as the sands of the sea or the stars of the sky. Think of it—when we ask for His help with a humble heart and a determination to obey, a whole universe of help opens to us!

(Harry Anderson, The Resurrected Jesus Christ, *© 1992 Intellectual Reserve, Inc. All rights reserved.)*

"It Is Finished"

Elder John H. Groberg

EASTER TIME IS a wonderful time to bear testimony of our Lord and Savior, Jesus Christ, to give gratitude for Him, to show our love for Him, and to increase our faith in Him.

I know He lives. I know He loves us. I know He is the Son of God. I know He is our Friend. I know that through Him—His creations, His Atonement, His Resurrection, and His Final Judgment—it is possible for all of us to return to our Father in Heaven and receive the incomparable gifts of the assurance of immortality, the opportunity for eternal life, and the endless joy that comes therefrom.

How can we adequately express our love and gratitude for all He has done and for all He continues to do for us? Jesus gives the answer: "If ye love me, keep my commandments"

Elder John H. Groberg is an emeritus member of the First Quorum of the Seventy.

(John 14:15). In other words, we show our love and express our gratitude by keeping His commandments, which is living according to the laws of truth that bring eternal life and joy.

Jesus is perfect. He loves His Father fully, keeps His commandments fully, and thereby experiences a fullness of joy. We are imperfect. We love Jesus but presently fall short of keeping His commandments fully. He understands this and wants to help us. He knows that as our obedience increases, our love increases, and as our love increases, our obedience increases even more; and that round continues on and on unto eventual perfection, which is the goal.

He has made it clear: "I would that ye should be perfect even as I, or your Father who is in heaven is perfect" (3 Nephi 12:48). This goal scares some of us, as we feel we simply cannot do it. We cannot do it on our own, but we can with His help. We are weak, but He is strong. How many rounds will it take? How much help will we need? A lot, but no matter what it takes, Jesus will be there to help us.

Moroni explains, "Come unto Christ, and be perfected in him, . . . and if ye . . . love God with all your might, mind and strength, then is his grace sufficient for you, that by his grace ye may be perfect in Christ" (Moroni 10:32). What a glorious promise! Think of it—eventually our love can be full. Our obedience can be full. Our joy can be full! We have a long way to go. He understands that even better than we do. He is not discouraged with our progress, even though we may be. Trust Him. He is perfect. He can cleanse us even from deep scarlet (see Isaiah 1:18). He can give us confidence, faith, and hope and take doubt, fear, and uncertainty from our hearts.

He is our ever-present Friend. He is aware of falling sparrows and failing individuals. He controls the universe and everything in it. The ways He can help us are as innumerable as the sands of the sea or the stars of the sky. Think of it—when we ask for His help with a humble heart and a determination to obey, a whole universe of help opens to us!

Let us anxiously respond to His gracious offer: "Verily I say unto you, my friends, . . . call upon me. . . . Draw near unto me and I will draw near unto you; seek me diligently and ye shall find me; ask, and ye shall receive; knock, and it shall be opened unto you" (D&C 88:62–63). As we seek and ask and knock, what will we receive? What will be opened unto us? Everything that is good, everything that lasts forever and everything that brings joy. We will receive strength from Him to live the eternal laws of truth. As we draw near to Him, we will know more surely that He is our Savior, our Helper, and our ever-faithful Friend.

I find, as I am sure you do, that drawing closer to the Savior and understanding better all He has done and continues to do for us is somewhat like climbing a mountain: the higher we go, the more we see. The more we see, the more there is to see. When we reach the top of one peak, we see other peaks rising beyond us—higher and more majestic—and realize that there is no end to His goodness. We find that His love is deeper, His mercy broader, His desire to help greater, and His power more all-encompassing than we can fathom. He lives. He loves us. He wants to help us. He is our Friend. This I know.

Oh how we should want to "always remember him and keep his commandments . . . that [we] may always have his Spirit to be with [us]" (D&C 20:77), as we regularly plead in the sacrament prayer.

Everything Jesus does and says is calculated to help us move toward eventual perfection in Him, round by round. A major part of remembering Him is remembering His words. In fact, He asks us to "live by *every word* that proceedeth forth from the mouth of God" (D&C 84:44; emphasis added). All of His words are important; all have deep meaning; all will help us.

JOURNEY TO GOLGOTHA

Come with me to Golgotha. As Jesus hung upon the cross in great physical, emotional, and spiritual pain, He continued to think of others and how He could help them. In love and compassion, he looked upon His mother and said, "Woman, behold thy son!" and to John, "Behold thy mother" (John 19:26, 27).

After this, I believe He reviewed everything He had promised to do, wanting to be sure that every prophecy concerning His vital mission in mortality had been fulfilled. I wonder if He remembered one more prophecy from Psalms, "And in my thirst they gave me vinegar to drink" (Psalm 69:21). For "Jesus knowing that *all things* were now accomplished, that the scripture might be fulfilled, saith, I thirst. . . . And they filled a

Even upon the cross, Christ reached out in compassion to others.
(James Tissot, The Death of Jesus.*)*

spunge with vinegar . . . and put it to his mouth" (John 19:28–29; emphasis added). Another prophecy fulfilled!

At this point I like to think that in some way—maybe a nod, a smile, an impression—He received the assurance from above that everything was in place, for the scripture continues, "When Jesus therefore had received the vinegar, he said, *It is finished*: and he bowed his head, and gave up the ghost" (John 19:30; emphasis added).

To His final mortal moment, He continued to help, to love, to teach, and to show us the way to eternal joy. It is difficult for me not to shed tears of gratitude as I contemplate this moment when His perfect mortal life came to a perfect conclusion.

What should we learn from those final words, "It is finished"? What was finished? His Atonement? His life? His work? He gives us the answer in the nineteenth section of the Doctrine and Covenants: "For behold, I, God, have suffered these things for all, . . . which suffering caused myself, even God, the greatest of all, to tremble because of pain, and to bleed at every pore, and to suffer both body and spirit— and would that I might not drink the bitter cup, and shrink— nevertheless, glory be to the Father, and I partook and *finished my preparations* unto the children of men" (D&C 19:16, 18–19; emphasis added).

So what was finished? His "preparations unto the children of men." He did not say everything was finished, but His preparations were, or that chapter of His life was. As the intense drama of possibly the greatest chapter in human history came to a close with those humble yet exultant words "It is finished," the next chapter was already opening.

ONGOING VOYAGE

When His Spirit left His body, Christ went to the spirit world and continued His work of teaching and helping others: "He organized his forces and appointed messengers, clothed with power and authority, and commissioned them to go forth

As the chapter of Christ's mortal ministry came to an end, a new chapter began. (Robert T. Barrett, Jesus Teaching in the Spirit World.*)*

and carry the light of the gospel to them that were in darkness, even to all the spirits of men" (D&C 138:30).

Not only was He personally moving from one chapter to the next, but He was teaching us by word and example that we are to see our assignments as chapters, and as one comes to a close, a new one opens. New chapters await us even beyond the grave, for as President Joseph F. Smith saw in vision, "The faithful elders [and sisters] of this dispensation, when they depart from mortal life, continue their labors in the preaching of the gospel of repentance and redemption . . . in the great world of the spirits of the dead" (D&C 138:57).

Everything Jesus has done, and continues to do, is to help us understand and live eternal truth so we may have eternal joy. Every assignment we receive is an opportunity for us to prepare to serve more effectively. Jesus' atoning sacrifice and resurrection was not the first chapter in helping us, nor will it be the last. Our birth was not our beginning, nor will our death be our end. All of life's experiences are to prepare us to better help others.

This principle was emblazoned on my mind and heart years ago when, as a young missionary in Tonga, I often traveled from island to island by sailboat.

Once after preaching for many days on several small islands, we were returning home one morning. We had no motor, no radio, no compass, just a small sail, an experienced captain, and lots of faith. We had hoped to be home that evening, but the wind turned contrary, the seas became rough, and it

We had no motor, no radio, no compass, just a small sail, an experienced captain, and lots of faith. (Courtesy of John H. Groberg.)

was obvious we would be on the ocean the rest of the day, through the night, and probably into the next day.

When night fell, it became cold and dark, and we were jolted and slapped by the heavy waves. I was miserable and couldn't sleep. When much of the night had passed, I went to visit with the captain. He was holding the main sail rope with one hand and the rudder pole with the other. A feeling of love washed over me as I sensed how intently he was concentrating on bringing us safely through the great deep.

As we visited, he told me of his deep reverence for God, whom he acknowledged as the Creator of the universe,

including the stormy sea we were on. Our visiting was inter-
rupted occasionally when large waves jostled us or strong gusts
of wind whipped the sail and tipped us precariously close to
the water. I asked if I could do anything to help, but he said he
was fine.

We visited until dawn, when we finally entered the calm
waters of Pangai Harbor. I marveled at his exquisite mind and
astonishing ability. He was humble yet confident. Though he
had no compass or radio, his mind, his body, his experience,
and his faith in God made our safe return possible.

As we neared the wharf, I thanked the captain and expressed my love and admiration for him. He nodded shyly,
but it was easy to tell that he too was grateful for our safe arrival. I threw my belongings over my shoulder, climbed onto
the wharf, and looked back at the captain. He was busy bailing
cans of bilgewater, cleaning the boat, and getting ready for his
next voyage.

Then it came to me: for the captain, that particular voyage was finished, but his journey continued. He had paid
attention, brought us home safely, and expanded his level of
experience for his coming voyages. Some of those voyages
would be smooth, some rough, most normal, but all doable.
The same is true of our journey through life. We are to fill our
assignments, pay attention, rely on the Lord, bring people
home safely, learn from our experiences, and prepare for our
next assignment or chapter, regardless of the storms or calms
we experience.

The work of redemption goes on and on in one great eternal round—voyage after voyage, assignment after assignment, chapter after chapter—and Jesus is always there to help.

I have asked two BYU students to sing the hymn "Jesus, Lover of My Soul." These words of Charles Wesley continue to plead for all of us:

> Jesus, lover of my soul,
> Let me to thy bosom fly,
> While the nearer waters roll,
> While the tempest still is high.
> Hide me, O my Savior, hide,
> Till the storm of life is past.
> Safe into the haven guide;
> Oh, receive my soul at last.
>
> Other refuge have I none;
> Hangs my helpless soul on thee.
> Leave, oh, leave me not alone;
> Still support and comfort me.
> All my trust on thee is stayed;
> All my help from thee I bring.
> Cover my defenseless head
> With the shadow of thy wing.[1]

When we feel His spirit, we feel His joy. We also feel His power and His desire to help us. Everything good comes through diligence and obedience to truth, as explained in this scripture: "Whatever principle of intelligence we attain unto in this life, it will rise with us in the resurrection. And if a person gains more knowledge and intelligence in this life through his *diligence* and *obedience* than another, he will have so much the advantage in the world to come" (D&C 130:18–19; emphasis added).

In the creation of the world, we see God move through chapters.

This process of moving from chapter to chapter and learning from each one is everywhere. For example, think of the creation of this world. The Lord worked hard the first day. Only when everything was working properly did He pronounce it "good" or "finished," and then He moved to the next day. He continued day after day with each assignment until He could pronounce the whole creation "good" or "finished."

Each day was a preparation for the next one. Who can say which day was the most important? Each day interrelates with and is dependent upon the others. So it is with our lives—our birth, our growth, our assignments, our challenges, our family, our death—all are important and relate to each other. Each chapter is necessary.

ETERNAL PROGRESSION IN FAMILIES

This same process is at the heart of the most important unit in eternity—the family. When a baby is born, the chapter of birth is finished, but we quickly realize that what was finished was but our preparations for that child. One chapter

Family provides some of the most important chapters in this life.

has closed, the next opened. Now we are parents and have the responsibility to help that child grow and learn and mature and understand. In the next chapter we teach, train, and nurture that child. We will likely start new chapters with other children, but now with more experience. And so it continues, chapter after chapter, round after round.

Occasionally I hear people say their family is finished, and I wonder exactly what they mean by this. In a spiritual sense, families are never finished. In a physical sense, there are limitations. The number or gender of children is not a critical factor. Prophets and other righteous people over the ages have had from none to few to many children.

We should not and cannot judge others. Everyone is unique. The process of bringing children into a family involves so many diverse factors of such a deep personal nature that only God can see through it all. He will give the right answers to those who humbly seek His counsel. The most critical factor is counseling together and with the Lord through prayer, then following the promptings of His Spirit.

In our day we may think we have control over many of these things, but we must remember that it is only God who has complete control. It is God to whom we must ultimately report—not a doctor, a parent, a professor, a social worker, or any other mortal. If we put personal limits on following the Savior and the promptings of His Spirit in any way, we put limits on the blessings we can receive from Him.

This life is not about our convenience but about our conversion—that is, our conversion from being a natural man or woman to becoming a man or woman of God by consistently following the promptings of His Spirit. God gives us the opportunity to change from a rather helpless mass of potential to a powerful force for doing good by giving us challenging assignments or chapters to fill. Upon asking, He gives us the help we need, including letting us know when we are ready to move to the next chapter. Peace, progress, and joy come from living according to God's will, not ours.

Is our responsibility to our children or our family ever finished? A particular chapter may be, but our journey never is.

Think of our exemplar, the Savior. Is His work ever finished? He explained to Moses, "I will show thee the workmanship of mine hands; but not all, for my works are without end, and also my words, for they *never cease*. . . . And as one earth shall pass away, and the heavens thereof even so shall another come; and

The work of the Savior and His creations never cease. (Orion Nebula, NASA/ JPL-Caltech/T. Megeath [University of Toledo] and M. Robberto [STScI].)

Lorenzo Snow taught important truths about the eternal nature of families.
(Courtesy of Church History Museum.)

there is *no end to my works, neither to my words*" (Moses 1:4, 38; emphasis added).

When a husband and wife qualify for the celestial kingdom, what is finished? Their preparation to begin a new chapter! President Lorenzo Snow taught this eternal process beautifully:

> When two Latter-day Saints are united together in marriage, promises are made to them concerning their offspring that reach from eternity to eternity. They are promised that they shall have the power and the right to govern and control and administer salvation and exaltation and glory to their offspring, worlds without end.... What else could man wish? A

man and a woman, in the other life, having celestial
bodies, free from sickness and disease, glorified and
beautified beyond description, standing in the midst
of their posterity, governing and controlling them,
administering life, exaltation and glory worlds
without end.[2]

This new chapter will be glorious but also overwhelming.
What a comfort to know that Jesus will always be there to help
us! We will not just start building or organizing alone. We will
continue to be taught "line upon line, precept upon precept,
here a little and there a little" (2 Nephi 28:30; see also D&C
98:12; 128:21). Each chapter has a purpose, and like a great
book, each chapter must be read and experienced so we can
see and understand the whole story.

ANOTHER CHAPTER

Sometimes we struggle with an assignment or have difficulty getting through just one day, let alone a whole chapter.
We may even secretly be glad when a particular assignment
is over and hope it never comes again. God understands our
feelings, but He also understands our potential and will continue to give us new opportunities that will increase our ability to help others, so long as we recognize and accept them. We
grow from faith to faith, and when we reach our extremities,
Jesus says in effect, "I will help you finish that chapter," much
as the angel from heaven strengthened Him in an hour of need
in the garden (see Luke 22:43).

When we struggle with any chapter, there is always help for us. (Carl Heinrich Bloch, Gethsemane, *© Intellectual Reserve Inc. All Rights Reserved.)*

If we quit on any chapter, we will not see the whole story or be fully prepared for the next one. We need to keep going, even when it hurts. It is not what we say or pray but what we do and sacrifice that "brings forth the blessings of heaven."[3]

Temple work is a vital part of many chapters. When we understand the eternal nature of temple work, we will make it a bigger part of our lives. The Savior constantly invites us to come unto Him, so just where does He want us to come? To where He is—His home, the holy temple. I know it pleases Him when we visit Him there often. I also know there is no end to the help we can receive from Him there.

As we move from chapter to chapter, we must learn to turn away from the idols and the idleness of this world and turn to the houses of the Lord and the essential work done there. Time spent in great and spacious buildings which are filled with the pride of the world yields little of eternal significance. Time spent in buildings which are filled with the Spirit of the

Temple work is a vital part of many chapters.
(Splorticus, Salt Lake Temple, Wikimedia.)

Lord, such as temples, can become as great and spacious and wide as all eternity. In them we can learn everything and go everywhere of eternal significance, for the Teacher there is the Creator of everything good and eternal. He loves us and wants to help us.

CALLS AND RELEASES

In addition to teaching us how to faithfully move from one chapter to the next, the Savior's words "It is finished" also teach us that calls and releases in His kingdom come from those in authority. We do not call or release ourselves, nor do we set the terms of service—God does. Jesus, though in great pain, waited until He was given to know "that all things were . . . accomplished" before He said, "It is finished" (John 19:28, 30). On our level, we must learn to do the same.

Years ago an older gentleman helped me understand this principle. As a young man, he had taken a teaching job in a small Latter-day Saint farming community. There were two major extended families in that area who did not get along. When the stake president called a bishop from one side, the other side stayed home from Church meetings. A year or so later, he called a bishop from the other side, and the first side stayed home.

Before long the stake president called this young school-teacher who belonged to neither side to be the bishop. He told the stake president he would accept the call if he also could be released in a year or so. To his surprise, the stake president responded, "If you are not a good bishop, I will release you sooner than that. This is a calling from the Lord, not me!"

He became the bishop, prayed, worked hard, and was blessed by the Lord. The family rifts gradually healed, and eventually everyone came back to church. He served as bishop for over fifteen years and then was called to be the stake president. He had a wonderful family and told me he felt his blessings came from serving according to the Lord's will, not his.

We must all learn this lesson. We do not choose where or how long we will serve. Some people love their missions or other callings so much they would like to stay longer. Others do not like their callings and would like to be released sooner. Only when the Lord, through His leaders, says, "It is finished," is that chapter over. Only then are we fully ready for the next chapter.

The Lord will direct us, like Brigham Young, to know when we might be ready for the next chapter. (Courtesy of Church History Museum.)

Brigham Young left his family and went on mission after mission and would have kept going, except the Lord through His prophet said, "My servant Brigham, it is no more required at your hand to leave your family as in times past, for *your offering is acceptable to me*. I have seen your labor and toil in journeyings for my name. I therefore command you to send my word abroad, and take especial care of your family from this time, henceforth and forever. Amen" (D&C 126:1–3; emphasis added).

The Prophet Joseph Smith seemed to move from chapter to chapter at an astonishing rate. Even though he was hounded and harried, he continued to work hard, wait patiently, and be faithful until the Lord called him home, stating in effect, "Your earthly mission is finished. You are now ready for the next chapter beyond the grave, where your voice will be heard by millions."

I marvel at many of the early-day, as well as present-day, brothers and sisters who have faithfully fulfilled difficult assignments. I pray we may all do likewise. We must leave it to God to say, "It is finished," because He understands everything, including our ability and potential, and we do not.

As we do things that *require* faith in the Lord, our faith in Him increases. We may not want to do some things, but if we sincerely try, He makes it possible for us to accomplish every assignment—be it building a boat, getting some brass plates, having a child, filling a calling, caring for someone with emotional or physical challenges, settling differences, overcoming anger, or any other difficult chapter. Remember that every assignment fulfilled, every act of love given, and every sacrifice made by us is but a tiny reflection of the Savior's unending sacrifice, love, and help.

The Prophet Joseph Smith.
(Alvin Gittins, © Intellectual Reserve, Inc. All rights reserved.)

Whenever I question the length or difficulty of any assignment, I try to remember the Savior hanging on the cross in great pain, yet continuing to help others until He received the assurance from above that His mortal mission was complete. Only then did He say, "It is finished." In the greatest act of love and sacrifice ever performed, Jesus defeated *all* the forces of evil and wrought an Atonement and a Resurrection for the eternal benefit and joy of all mankind. What an example! I pray that each of us, like the Savior, will accept every assignment or chapter offered us and continue faithful in it until someone in authority says, "It is finished."

As we move from chapter to chapter, we become better prepared and able to do what President Thomas S. Monson so sincerely and consistently asks us to do—help those in need in every possible way. As we live by the Savior's words, we show our love and gratitude for Him and stay firmly on the path to becoming more like Him and eventually becoming perfect in Him!

President Thomas S. Monson.

I testify that Jesus lives, that He loves us, that He helps us, that He is at home in His temple, and that He is our Friend. I testify that Joseph Smith is the prophet of the Restoration and that Thomas S. Monson is God's mouthpiece on the earth today. I leave my love and blessings with you, in the name of Jesus Christ, amen.

(Photograph by Craig Dimond, © Intellectual Reserve, Inc. All rights reserved.)

NOTES

1. Charles Wesley, "Jesus, Lover of My Soul," *Hymns* (Salt Lake City: The Church of Jesus Christ of Latter-day Saints, 1985), no. 102.
2. Lorenzo Snow, *Deseret News Weekly*, April 3, 1897, 481.
3. William W. Phelps, "Praise to the Man," *Hymns*, no. 27.

Generally at Easter time we talk about Christ's sacrifice and what it means to us. But I should like to focus more on what the Atonement meant for Jesus. . . . Yes, Jesus was the Son of God, but He was also a man. . . . It was not just the Son of God who went through that first Easter week, it was also the man Jesus. And knowing that has relevance for us today.

(*Adam Abrams,* Gethsemane, © *2008 Adam Abrams.*)

What the Atoning Sacrifice Meant for Jesus

Elder Gerald N. Lund

It is always a challenge to talk or write about the Atonement of Jesus Christ. First of all, it is infinite in its scope. It is the most profound and pivotal event in all of eternity. And we are so totally and utterly finite. We can but glimpse its importance and come only to a small understanding of its full meaning for us.

Another problem is the sheer volume of the record of that week. Christ's ministry lasted three years, or 156 weeks. Thus the final week of His life constitutes only two-tenths of one percent of His ministry, yet that week occupies fully one-third of the total pages of the four Gospels. In a few short pages, I could not even recount the events of that most significant of all weeks in history; therefore, I have chosen to take a somewhat different approach to Easter Week.

Elder Gerald N. Lund is a released member of the Seventy.

Generally at Easter time we talk about Christ's sacrifice and what it means to us. But I should like to focus more on what the Atonement meant for Jesus. Sometimes we forget that side of the story. Yes, Jesus was the Son of God, but He was also a man. He had a body like ours that needed food and sleep. He had personality and character traits. If He walked too far in one day, His feet would blister. If He hit His thumb while working in the carpenter's shop, it hurt like fury, and the thumbnail eventually turned black.

It was not just the Son of God who went through that first Easter week, it was also the man Jesus. And knowing that has relevance for us today. So I shall draw just a few glimpses from the scriptures of what those final days must have meant for Him. In doing so, it is my hope that we will deepen our appreciation not only for what He did, but *for what He was.*

"THE WILL OF THE SON BEING SWALLOWED UP IN THE WILL OF THE FATHER"

When Abinadi gave his final defense before the wicked King Noah, the prophet testified of the coming Messiah and the atonement He would make for us. One statement he made provides a profound insight into the Savior's personality and character. "He shall be led, crucified, and slain, the flesh becoming subject even unto death, the will of the Son being swallowed up in the will of the Father" (Mosiah 15:7). That aspect of Christ's life was true not just in those final hours, but it was the defining statement of His nature.

One of the greatest blessings we have in life is agency—the right to choose what we shall do, where we live, how we act, what we believe. If we grow weary of our employment, we can choose to find other work. If we do not like our neighborhood, we can move. When we find the monotony or burdens of life pressing in, we call in sick or go on vacation or simply just quit and give up. In short, we are free to follow our will. The Savior also had agency, but His will, His wants, His desires, His wishes always came second. As He said in the Garden of Gethsemane, "Not as I will, but as thou wilt" (Matthew 26:39). On another occasion, some of His enemies asked, "Who art thou?" (John 8:25). His answer reflected His total commitment to His Father. He said, "I do nothing of myself; but as my Father hath taught me; . . . I do always those things that please him" (John 8:28–29).

That submission was the hallmark of His life, and had it not been so, the Atonement would never have become reality. Let us think of that the next time we sing, "I'm trying to be like Jesus" or "Lord, I would follow thee."[1]

"WHY HAST THOU FORSAKEN ME?"

Here is a brief but powerful insight from the New Testament record. One of the most haunting moments occurred on the cross when Jesus suddenly cried out, "My God, my God, why hast thou forsaken me?" (Matthew 27:46). Surely much of the ministry of Jesus involved a certain degree of loneliness. Which of His contemporaries could possibly understand what He was and who He was? How many times was He scorned and mocked, ridiculed and reviled? Sometimes even

His closest disciples misunderstood what He said or why He did the things He did. In one sense, He was always alone. But there was one great comfort through all of that. Maybe no one else fully understood Him, but His Father did. At least twice during his ministry, He made specific statements about His relationship with the Father, and it is clear that He drew great comfort from this knowledge.

In John 8:29, He said, "He that sent me is with me: the Father hath not left me alone; for I do always those things that please him." A short time later, He said to the Twelve: "Behold, the hour cometh, yea, is now come, that ye shall be scattered, every man to his own, and shall leave me alone: and yet I am not alone, because the Father is with me" (John 16:32).

As Christ left the Upper Room with His disciples, He seems to have had a clear idea of the ordeal which lay ahead. But He evidently did not foresee this one aspect of the coming trial. It seems to have come as a shock that in that terrible final hour, He was left utterly alone. Even the Father, who had never before left Him alone, withdrew His presence from Him. Elder James E. Talmage described that moment thus:

> What mind of man can fathom the significance of that awful cry? It seems, that in addition to the fearful suffering incident to crucifixion, the agony of Gethsemane had recurred, intensified beyond human power to endure. In that bitterest hour the dying Christ was alone, alone in most terrible reality. That the supreme sacrifice of the Son might

be consummated in all its fulness, the Father seems to have withdrawn the support of His immediate Presence, leaving to the Savior of men the glory of complete victory over the forces of sin and death.[2]

What it meant for Him at that moment is beyond our capacity to understand. Judging from the anguish, at that point even He did not understand. Later He would understand and use that understanding to succor us. There are times in almost every person's life when the burdens and anguish become so great that we too cry out, as the Prophet Joseph did from Liberty Jail, "O God, where art thou?" (D&C 121:1). And after His ordeal on the cross, the Savior can answer: "All of these things shall give thee experience, and shall be for thy good. The Son of Man hath descended below them all. Art thou greater than he?" (D&C 122:7–8).

"ABBA, FATHER"

Three of the four Gospel writers—Matthew, Mark, and Luke—include the account of the Savior's heart-wrenching prayer in the Garden of Gethsemane, where He pled with the Father to remove the terrible cup that He was about to drink. However, Mark adds one detail that is unique to his Gospel. He says that Jesus began His prayer with the words, "Abba, Father" (Mark 14:36). *Abba* is an Aramaic word which Mark chose not to translate into Greek. It is one of the words for "father." So why not just render the passage as "Father, Father"? Why leave an Aramaic word in an English translation?

Generally, translators leave in something from the original language because there is no good equivalent in the target language, or because if there is an equivalent, significant nuances of meaning are lost in translation. In this passage, the Greek text actually uses two different words for father, *abba* and *pater.* In his extensive work on New Testament word studies, W. E. Vine differentiates between *abba* and *pater* in this way: "'Abba' is the word framed by the lips of infants, and betokens unreasoning trust; 'father' [*pater*] expresses an intelligent apprehension [or understanding] of the relationship."[3] In other words, *pater* is the more formal term of address, typically used as children mature and grow to adulthood. But *abba* is the more intimate and affectionate form used by small children. Our equivalent in English would be "papa" or "daddy."[4]

Had the translators rendered the passage literally as "Daddy, Father," or "Papa, Father," it would seem a bit jarring to us. We do not address our Heavenly Father in such casual or familiar terms. One scholar explained it in these terms: "Probably to guard against the appearance of too great a familiarity, the writers of the New Testament, instead of using the Greek word, [*papa*] retained the foreign form *Abba* to give greater emphasis and dignity."[5]

But the fact that *abba* was used by the Savior in His hour of greatest need is of great significance. He spoke to His Father with the familiarity of a child for an adoring and adored parent, but at the same time He also used the more formal, respectful title. Both terms reveal the depth and breadth of their relationship. That simple addition by Mark provides a tender insight into their relationship which only adds greater meaning to that sacred moment.

However, it does much more than that. It reveals something about our own relationship with God that is of prime importance. Note the words of Paul the Apostle: "For as many as are led by the Spirit of God, they are the sons of God. For ye have . . . received the Spirit of adoption, whereby we cry, Abba, Father. The Spirit itself beareth witness with our spirit, that we are the children of God" (Romans 8:14–16). In other words, when we become the sons and daughters of God and are spiritually born again, then we shall have that same intimate but respectful relationship, and it shall be our privilege to call upon God as "Abba, Father."

A BROKEN HEART

The Gospel of John is unique in many ways, containing things which Matthew, Mark, and Luke did not include in their Gospels. In describing that horrible day when Jesus was nailed to the cross, John adds one short comment that is not found in the other Gospels but which gives a truly significant insight into Christ's death.

We often speak of Jesus being crucified, or say that He died on the cross. Indeed, the cross has become almost a universal symbol of His death in the Christian world. What is not as well known is that it is not likely that crucifixion was what killed Jesus.

It is not likely that crucifixion was what killed Jesus.
(*James Tissot,* The Confession of Saint Longinus.)

We know that crucifixion was used by the Romans to inflict the maximum amount of pain and suffering by prolonging death. The wounds inflicted by the nails were not fatal, and, though excruciatingly painful, they brought relatively little loss of blood. In a healthy person, death on the cross usually did not come any sooner than forty-eight hours, and in some cases, life persisted for a day or two longer than that. Usually the actual cause of death was a combination of hunger, shock, thirst, infection, exhaustion, and exposure.

A few hours after the Crucifixion, the Jewish leaders begged Pilate to take Jesus and the two others down from the cross because the high holy days of Passover were beginning. The common method for hastening death was to break both of the victim's legs by striking the shins with a heavy mallet. This additional shock, coupled with the removal of their ability to support themselves to some degree with their feet, brought rapid death.

When the soldiers arrived at Golgotha, they found the two thieves still alive and broke their legs. But to their astonishment, Jesus was already dead, even though it had only been three hours. Evidently, one of the soldiers, either to make sure that Jesus was dead, or to kill Him if He was not, thrust a spear into the Savior's side. John, who witnessed this, records, "And forthwith came there out blood and water. And he [i.e., John himself] that saw it bare record, and his record is true: and he knoweth that he saith true, that ye might believe" (John 19:34–35).

Talmage comments on this unusual statement of John's:

> If the soldier's spear was thrust into the left side of the Lord's body and actually penetrated the heart, the outrush of "blood and water" observed by John is further evidence of a cardiac rupture; for it is known that in the rare instances of death resulting from a breaking of any part of the wall of the heart, blood accumulates within the pericardium, and there undergoes a change by which the corpuscles separate as a partially clotted mass from the almost

> colorless, watery serum. . . . Great mental stress,
> poignant emotion either of grief or joy, and intense
> spiritual struggle are among the recognized causes
> of heart rupture.[6]

In short, it appears that the actual cause of the Savior's death was a broken heart, caused not by crucifixion but by the tremendous weight of sorrow and suffering He had endured in order to pay the price for sin.

Once again in the personal details of Christ's sacrifice there is profound relevance for us. The Apostle Paul likened our attempts to put away the natural man, or the old man of sin, as Paul called it, to the Crucifixion in these words: "Know ye not, that so many of us as were baptized into Jesus Christ were baptized into his death? . . . Knowing this, that our old man is crucified with him, that the body of sin might be destroyed, that henceforth we should not serve sin" (Romans 6:3, 6).

Clearly, Paul speaks metaphorically here, for we do not have to literally die to give up sin—only the natural or sinful part has to be put away. Knowing that Christ did not suffer death from the Crucifixion but from a broken heart, His example becomes the model for how we overcome the natural man.

To the Nephites, the resurrected Christ said, "Ye shall offer for a sacrifice unto me a broken heart and a contrite spirit. And whoso cometh unto me with a broken heart and a contrite spirit, him will I baptize with fire and with the Holy Ghost" (3 Nephi 9:20). To the Saints of our generation, He said, "Thou shalt offer a sacrifice unto the Lord thy God in righteousness, even that of a broken heart and a contrite spirit" (D&C 59:8). This process, which is called being "born again," requires that there first be a sincere and lasting repentance. But in what way is repentance like unto having a broken heart?

Once again we are indebted to Paul for the answer. Speaking to the Corinthians, he said, "Now I rejoice, . . . that ye sorrowed to repentance: for ye were made sorry after a godly manner. . . . For godly sorrow worketh repentance to salvation not to be repented of [or abandoned]: but the sorrow of the world worketh death" (2 Corinthians 7:9–10).

There are many ways in which a person can be sorry for doing wrong. We can feel sorry because we are caught and suffer punishment. We can regret that our foolish actions bring highly unpleasant consequences with them. For example, Mormon described the sorrowing of his people in those last terrible days before their destruction as the result of the fact that "the Lord would not always suffer them to take happiness in sin" (Mormon 2:13).

President Ezra Taft Benson defined godly sorrow and linked it directly to the concept of a broken heart:

> True repentance involves a change of heart and not just a change of behavior (see Alma 5:13). Part of this mighty change of heart is to feel godly sorrow for our sins. This is what is meant by a broken heart and a contrite spirit. . . .
>
> Godly sorrow is a gift of the Spirit. It is a deep realization that our actions have offended our Father

and our God. It is the sharp and keen awareness that our behavior caused the Savior, He who knew no sin, even the greatest of all, to endure agony and suffering. Our sins caused Him to bleed at every pore. This very real mental and spiritual anguish is what the scriptures refer to as having "a broken heart and a contrite spirit" (D&C 20:37). Such a spirit is the absolute prerequisite for true repentance.[7]

I should like to repeat one part of that statement: Godly sorrow "is a deep realization that our actions have offended our Father and our God. . . . This very real mental and spiritual anguish is what the scriptures refer to as having 'a broken heart and a contrite spirit.'"

What a beautiful and marvelous similitude! When Christ took sin upon Himself and suffered for it as if He were Himself guilty of it all, His sorrow and suffering were such that His great heart broke, and He died. And as we truly seek to put off the natural man, the sinful man that dwells inside our hearts, we emulate His example. When we realize that we have offended God's perfect holiness, that our actions are part of what added to Christ's suffering, the Spirit creates in us such a deep and piercing sorrow that it is likened unto having a broken heart.

THE CONDESCENSION OF GOD

These few brief insights—Christ's will being swallowed up in the will of the Father, the Savior's agonized cry from the cross, addressing God as "Abba, Father," and dying from a broken heart—lead us to another profound aspect of Christ's atoning sacrifice. It is what is called in the scriptures "the condescension of God." Twice in Nephi's great vision, an angel used that phrase—once just before Nephi was shown the birth of Jesus, and once as he was shown the trial and death of Jesus (see 1 Nephi 11:16, 26). Let us examine how these two aspects of Christ's life show His condescension.

The condescension of His birth. Let us again ask the question that sets the theme for this address. When Jesus left the premortal existence and came to earth, we know what it meant for us, but what did that mean *for Him?* Think about that for a moment. In the premortal life, Jesus was the Firstborn of the Father. Of all the countless billions of the spirit children of our Father, He was the first to be given a spirit body. His intelligence was the greatest of all. He then went on to serve as the great Creator, acting under the direction of the Father.

Let us consider just that aspect of Christ's premortal role. While there are several scriptures which attest to Christ's role as the Creator, it is in the Book of Moses that we are shown the extent of His role in the creation: "And worlds without number have I created; and I also created them for mine own purpose; and by the Son I created them, which is mine Only Begotten . . . and innumerable are they unto man. . . . The heavens, they are many, and they cannot be numbered unto man; . . . and there is no end to my works." (Moses 1:33, 35, 37–38).

Later in the book, we find these astonishing words of Enoch: "And were it possible that man could number the particles of the earth, yea, millions of earths like this, it would not be a beginning to the number of thy creations" (Moses 7:30).

To help you better appreciate the staggering enormity of that statement, let us consider only one tiny indicator of how vastly enormous that number would be. Imagine, if you can, the number of just one kind of particle we find on the earth, what we call a grain of sand. How many grains of sand would there be if you could count every grain on every beach, in every desert, in every gravel pit and river sandbar around the world? And that would not even be a beginning to the number of His creations.

Using a microscope, a telescope, or the naked eye, everywhere we look we see the complexity, the enormity, the beauty and the wonder of the creations of God. I briefly note only a few.

- There are over fifty thousand different species of spiders, including one that spins its web beneath the water and uses it like a diving bell, one that can jump forty times its own length from a standing position, or the bolas spider, which attaches a sticky blob to a single strand of webbing, then hurls it at passing moths, much like a fisherman casting for fish.

- With the great Mount Palomar telescope in California, astronomers can count over a million galaxies in the bowl of the Big Dipper. Not stars. *Galaxies* of stars.

- The lowly ant can lift as much as fifty times its own weight and carry it for some distance. That is the equivalent of a two-hundred-pound man bench pressing ten thousand pounds, or five tons.
- The trunk of an elephant is strong enough to lift a six-hundred-pound log and delicate enough to pick up a coin from a sidewalk.
- The design and colors in the tail feathers of the peacock are a marvelous work of art.
- The world produces enough food to feed six billion people every day.
- The human heart beats an average of fifty thousand times a day, or about one and a half billion times in a lifetime.
- The human fetus begins as a single sperm and egg, and in just under nine months develops into a fully formed human being.
- As part of that development, when the fetus is just seven weeks along, it begins to develop brains cells. At that point it is only one and half inches long and weighs less than half an ounce, but it produces new brains cells at the rate of more than one hundred thousand times every minute, or sixteen hundred new cells every second!

The miracles of creation are omnipresent and stunning in their wonder. And all of this was done under the power and direction of the Son of God. That was the station and status of the premortal Jesus. And He left all of that glory and power and perfection and took upon Himself the body of a mortal, subject to pain and weariness, hunger and thirst, blisters and boils and viruses—and death. To willingly undergo the transformation from godhood to manhood was indeed an act of tremendous condescension.

The condescension of His trial and crucifixion. But that is only one manifestation of Christ's condescension. In his vision, Nephi saw "the Lamb of God, that he was taken by the people; yea, the Son of the everlasting God was judged of the world; and I saw and bear record. And I, Nephi, saw that he was lifted up upon the cross and slain for the sins of the world" (1 Nephi 11:32–33). The irony in that statement is incredible. Wicked and evil and puny men put the Son of the God on trial and sent Him to the cross for blasphemy and thought that they were doing God a service when they did so.

This part of the vision so profoundly influenced Nephi, that later he referred to those last hours of Christ in this way: "And the world, because of their iniquity, shall judge him to be a thing of naught; wherefore they scourge him, and he suffereth it; and they smite him, and he suffereth it. Yea, they spit upon him, and he suffereth it, because of his loving kindness and his long-suffering towards the children of men" (1 Nephi 19:9).

Remember who and what Jesus was before He came to earth. Also consider the miracles that He had wrought during His mortal ministry—healing the blind, stilling the storm, cleansing the leper, making crippled limbs function, raising a man who had been dead for four days. In that context, think of this. When the Son of God was brought before those arrogant and hypocritical leaders of the Jews, they made mock of Him. They dared Him to prophesy, cuffed Him with the back of their hands, and one even spit into His face. And Jesus suffered it!

Knowing who He was and the power at His command, at any moment of that terrible ordeal, He could have uttered a single word and brought down fire on the Sanhedrin as He did on the priests of Baal, or utterly destroyed Jerusalem as He did Sodom or Gomorrah. Or for that matter, since He had the power to create the earth, surely He had the power to destroy it as well. But He chose not to. He chose to endure the humiliation, the pain, the spittle running down His cheek, and, as Nephi said, "he suffereth it" because of His great love for us. Is it any wonder that the angel said to Nephi as he witnessed these scenes in vision, "Behold the condescension of God!" (1 Nephi 11:26).

HOW DO WE EVER REPAY SUCH A GIFT?

As we consider these various insights into what the Atonement meant for Jesus personally, we are led to exclaim, "What could I ever possibly do to repay the Father and the Son for all of this?" It is a valid question, and one born of humility. But in reality, the answer is that we can do nothing that would repay God and Christ for what they did. In the true meaning of the word *repay*, what can we give to God that He does not already have? How can the finite repay the infinite? It simply is not possible.

But that, of course, does not imply that we can do nothing. There are offerings we can make which will be acceptable to them and received with joy. Elder Talmage, who spent much of his life studying the life and work of the Savior, answered this dilemma in a wonderful parable which he called "The Parable of the Grateful Cat."

He tells the true story of a famous naturalist in England who was to be honored for his scientific achievements. He was invited to a great country estate where the awards were to be given. The morning after his arrival, as was his custom, he arose early and went out for a walk in the grounds. As he approached a millpond, he came across two boys, children of servants who served the wealthy estate owners. The boys were in the process of drowning kittens in weighted sacks in the pond.

As it turned out, the mistress of the estate had an old mother cat who had given birth to another litter of kittens. While the lady of the estate wanted to keep the mother cat, she did want any more cats around and so asked the boys to get rid of the kittens. When the naturalist arrived on the scene, two of the five kittens were already in the water and drowning. The mother cat was nearby, running frantically back and forth, mewing piteously as she watched her little ones being disposed of. The naturalist intervened, paying the boys and promising them that they would not get into trouble if they let him take the remaining kittens back to his cottage. Elder Talmage describes what happened next: "The mother cat . . . recognized the man as the deliverer of her three children. . . . As he carried the kittens she trotted along—sometimes following, sometimes alongside, occasionally rubbing against him with grateful yet mournful purrs."

What followed the next day formed the basis of the parable: "The gentleman was seated in his parlor on the ground floor, in the midst of a notable company. Many people had gathered to do honor to the distinguished naturalist. The cat came in. In her mouth she carried a large, fat mouse, not dead, but still feebly struggling under the pains of torturous capture. She laid her panting and well-nigh expiring prey at the feet of the man who had saved her kittens. What think you of the offering, and of the purpose that prompted the act? A live mouse, fleshy and fat! Within the cat's power of possible estimation and judgment it was a superlative gift."

Now comes the lesson for us. Elder Talmage concludes with this: "Are not our offerings to the Lord—our tithes and our other freewill gifts—as thoroughly unnecessary to His needs as was the mouse to the scientist? . . . Thanks be to God that He gages the offerings and sacrifices of His children by the standard of their physical ability and honest intent rather than by . . . His esteemed station. Verily He is God with us; and He both understands and accepts our motives and righteous desires. Our need to serve God is incalculably greater than His need for our service."[8]

So what if the mouse brought no personal profit to the scientist? What if he was far above and far removed from the gift of a half-expired rodent? Surely his heart swelled with a deep and lasting joy at such an offering from the mother cat.

While it is true that we cannot repay God in the strictest sense of that word, there are offerings we can make that will be pleasing to Him. Here are four that the scriptures suggest are especially pleasing to God.

1. *Acknowledgment.* In the fifty-ninth section of the Doctrine and Covenants we are told, "And in nothing doth man offend God, or against none is his wrath kindled, save those who confess not his hand in all things" (v. 21). How quick is mankind to blame God for the natural disasters and sufferings we find in the world, yet how slow to acknowledge His hand in the myriad goodness of life. For the Lord to say that such thoughtlessness kindles His wrath is an indication of how important this acknowledgment is to Him and to us.

2. *Acceptance.* Later in the Doctrine and Covenants the Lord says this: "For what doth it profit a man if a gift is bestowed upon him, and he receive not the gift? Behold, he rejoices not in that which is given unto him, neither rejoices in him who is the giver of the gift" (D&C 88:33). How tragic that God so loved the world that He gave His Only Begotten Son, and the world is so blind and apathetic that it does not care. It turns away from the gift as if it were of no consequence whatever.

3. *Gratitude.* Several scriptures speak of the importance of gratitude. In Psalms we read "Serve the Lord with gladness: come before his presence with singing. . . . Enter into his gates with thanksgiving, and into his courts with praise: be thankful

unto him, and bless his name" (Psalm 100:2, 4). In a modern revelation we are commanded to "thank the Lord thy God in all things" (D&C 59:7). Gratitude, which is expressed in both word and deed, is another way of acknowledging what God has done for us and accepting the gifts He extends to us.

4. *Remembrance*. Finally there is remembrance, which is perhaps the most important of them all. Some years ago, after I taught a class on the Atonement, one of the members, who was a practicing physician, handed me an article. He said, "I think in light of what you taught us tonight, you will find this interesting." To my surprise, the article was from a medical journal called *Private Practice* and had nothing to do with religion, let alone Christ. In fact, it was an article about a mountain climbing school in Colorado that catered to doctors and other professional people. I was puzzled as I read through it, wondering why he had given it to me.

Then I came to something he had marked near the end of the article, and then I understood. It was another parable, of sorts, though it was not written with that intent. The author of the article was interviewing the man who ran the climbing school, whose name was Czenkusch. They were talking about one of the key techniques in rock climbing, known as "belaying." To put it simply, belaying is the process by which one climber secures another climber so that he or she can safely ascend the rock face. This is done by having the lead climber loop a rope around his or her own body, then keeping the rope taut as the climber ascends so if there is a slip, the person on belay does not fall.

Understanding that much, here then is the paragraph that the doctor had marked for me:

> Belaying has brought Czenkusch his best and worse moments in climbing. Czenkusch once fell from a high precipice, yanking out three mechanical supports and pulling his belayer off a ledge. He was stopped, upside down, 10 feet from the ground when his spread-eagled belayer arrested the fall with the strength of his outstretched arms. "Don saved my life," says Czenkusch. "How do you respond to a guy like that? Give him a used climbing rope for Christmas? No, you remember him. You always remember him."[9]

What a marvelous analogy! The Savior, by the power of His own life and infinite sacrifice, is able to arrest our fall and save us from death. How do we thank Him for that? A new climbing rope is not any more needed by God than a fat field mouse. But we can vow that we shall never forget the gift. And in fact, this principle is so important that God asks to put ourselves under covenant each and every week that we will always remember Him.

There are thirty-three verses in the standard works that specifically describe the ordinance of the sacrament. The words *remember* and *remembrance* are used twenty-three times in those

verses. For example, when Jesus visited the Nephites and in-
stituted the sacrament among them, He told them to partake
of the bread and wine "in remembrance" of His body and His
blood, and four different times He said, "Always remember
me" (3 Nephi 18:7, 11). That pattern is repeated in the sacramen-
tal prayers we offer each Sunday. With the bread, we witness
to the Father that we are "*willing* to . . . always remember him,"
and with the water, we witness that we "*do* always remember
him" (D&C 20:77, 79; emphasis added). And the promise is that
if we honor those covenants, then another inestimable gift becomes ours: We will always have His Spirit to be with us.

What is it about the simple act of remembrance that carries
such much significance? Because it is in remembering that we
are impelled to action. Remembrance becomes the motivating,
driving force that helps us strive to be more like the Father and
the Son. It is in remembrance that we find the power to be a
better person. Jesus taught the disciples, "If ye love me, keep
my commandments" (John 14:15). When we remember all that
the Father and Son have done for us, it rekindles and renews
our love for them, and that renewed love becomes a powerful
agent for change.

Let me close with a poem that is a gentle and yet poignant
reminder of the importance of remembrance, especially at this
Easter season.

> When Jesus came to Golgotha they hanged him on
> a tree,

They drove great nails through hands and feet,
and made a Calvary;

They crowned Him with a crown of thorns, red
were his wounds, and deep,

For those were crude and cruel days, and human
flesh was cheap.

When Jesus came to [our town] they simply
passed Him by,

They never hurt a hair of Him, they only let Him
die;

For men had grown more tender, and they would
not give Him pain,

They only just passed down the street, and left
Him in the rain.[10]

When I first began asking myself the question, "What did
the Atonement mean for Jesus personally?" I found my understanding and appreciation for Him and for what He did
increasing in great measure. I found my gratitude deepening,
my understanding expanding, and my heart softening. So
may we, at this Easter season, remember the personal side of
the Atonement as well as the universal side. It was Jesus the
man who had to actually carry out the mission of Jesus the
Christ and totally submit His will to God the Father. Who can
adequately describe what that meant for Him? But thanks be
to the Lord that He drank of that bitter cup and, in the end, is
able to say, "I partook and finished my preparations unto the
children of men" (D&C 19:19). May we recommit ourselves

to acknowledging His gift, accepting it with gratitude and always remembering Him.

© Intellectual Reserve, Inc.

NOTES

1. Janice Kapp Perry, "I'm Trying to Be like Jesus," *Children's Songbook* (Salt Lake City: The Church of Jesus Christ of Latter-day Saints, 1985), 78–79; Susan Evans McCloud, "Lord, I Would Follow Thee," *Hymns* (Salt Lake City: The Church of Jesus Christ of Latter-day Saints, 1985), no. 220.

2. James E. Talmage, *Jesus the Christ* (Salt Lake City: Deseret Book, 1962), 612.

3. W. E. Vine, *An Expository Dictionary of New Testament Words* (Nashville: T. Nelson, 1981), 9.

4. Tremper Longman and David E. Garland, *The Expositor's Bible Commentary* (Grand Rapids, MI: Zondervan, 2005), 8:764; 10:473.

5. Samuel Fallows, Andrew Constantinides Zenos, and Herbert Lockwood Willett, eds., *The Popular and Critical Bible Encyclopædia and Scriptural Dictionary* (Chicago: Howard-Severance, 1912), 10.

6. Talmage, *Jesus the Christ*, 620.

7. *The Teachings of Ezra Taft Benson* (Salt Lake City: Bookcraft, 1988), 71–72.

8. James E. Talmage, "The Parable of the Grateful Cat," *Improvement Era*, August 1916, 875–76.

9. Quoted in Eric G. Anderson, "The Vertical Wilderness," *Private Practice*, November 1979, 21.

10. "Indifference," in *The Unutterable Beauty: The Collected Poetry of G. A. Studdert Kennedy* (London: Hodder and Stoughton, 1928), 24.

Repentance empowers us, actually revealing to us our real worth in the eyes of God and showing us that we are worthy of his atoning power and that the promised transformation is real.

"To Them Gave He Power to Become"

Daniel L. Belnap

John describes Christ's mortal ministry in John 12:1 in the following manner: "But as many as received him, to them gave he power to become the sons of God, even them that believe on his name." Though no mention is made of the sacrifice in Gethsemane or of his life-giving death on the cross or of his sublime Resurrection, this verse nonetheless reveals the purpose behind all three of these. The transformation of those who would live in such a manner as to become the sons and daughters of God is of course the very reason for the plan of salvation, but this verse does more than simply speak of Christ's necessary role in our physical transformation into exalted beings. It also speaks to Christ's role as a deliverer of

---

Daniel L. Belnap is assistant professor of ancient scripture at Brigham Young University.

knowledge concerning who we are and what we are to become, knowledge that is just as necessary to our salvation as the overcoming of death.

The well-known aphorism "Knowledge is power" certainly resonates with the doctrines of the Church. Speaking of the relationship between knowledge and power, the Prophet Joseph Smith taught, "God has more power than all other beings, because he has greater knowledge,"[1] establishing that divine action is the result of divine knowledge. The relationship between knowledge and power stems from the nature of knowledge itself, which is awareness—a cognitive, conscious awareness of something. As we become aware of a thing—be it an object, a concept, or a being—we are able to evaluate it and to become aware of the different aspects of that thing. This allows us to determine our relationship with that object, concept, or being and then act or react accordingly. Knowing the relationship between knowledge and power explains why we seek for more knowledge and why this search is essential for salvation; as Joseph Smith has stated, "A man is saved no faster than he gets knowledge."[2] With this in mind, there are three things that one must know to experience the transformation described by John: (1) what it means to be a son or daughter of God, (2) that such a designation is indeed possible to achieve, and (3) how Christ and his sacrifice made this possible to acquire.

BECOMING A SON OR DAUGHTER OF GOD

Fortunately, the doctrine of what it means to be a son or daughter of God is found throughout the scriptures. The Apostle Paul considered this theme in his letter to the Romans as he sought to reconcile the cultural differences between the Jewish and Gentile converts and establish the covenantal oneness that should define the disciples of Christ. In Romans 8:14 he revealed that "as many are led by the Spirit of God, they are the sons of God," thus defining the son or daughter of God not merely as one who is his literal offspring but as one who demonstrates fidelity to the covenant established by God. In other words, the recognition of one as a son or daughter of God is based on one's living righteously and interacting with the Holy Ghost. Those "who are led by the Spirit" become "heirs of God, joint-heirs with Christ" (Romans 8:17). Similarly, Doctrine and Covenants 76 reveals that those who "receive the Holy Spirit . . . and who overcome by faith . . . are they into whose hands the Father has given all things. . . . They are gods, even the sons of God—wherefore, all things are theirs" (vv. 52–53, 55, 58–59). Thus, becoming a son or daughter of God means that we have lived in such a manner to have received the right to our divine inheritance, all that our Father hath.

Yet the value of sonship or daughtership is more than a future inheritance; there are blessings of this state that can be experienced in the here and now. Before receiving the vision recorded in Moses 1, Moses was told by God, "Thou art my son; wherefore look and I will show thee the workmanship of mine hands" (Moses 1:4). Similarly, Abraham was told, "My son, my son (and his hand was stretched out), behold I will show you all [my works]" (Abraham 3:12). In both cases, it is their relationship as sons to God that allows them to receive the revelations described above. The relationship between sonship and revelation is made particularly clear in Moses with the term "wherefore." Because Moses was a son of God, he could see, if he chose to do so, the workmanship of God. Thus, becoming a son or daughter opens one to new revelatory experiences, even witnessing all that the Father has done in the here and now.

ACHIEVING THIS STATE

As incredible as the doctrine of sonship may be, for this doctrine to have any power one must also know that such a designation is achievable, is not merely possible but doable. It is impossible to obtain this knowledge without the Atonement, not because it is difficult to comprehend based on the process described, but because one cannot achieve this state without the transformation of self made possible through the Atonement. Unfortunately, the world tells us that this knowledge does not exist at all and that one who seeks for it is a fool. My wife and I were on a plane to California a few years ago, and we overheard a conversation between a father and his young son. The boy had just twisted off a soft drink cap and asked his dad if he had won a contest the drink was offering. His father replied, "No, you're a loser," to which his son immediately piped up, "I'm not a loser. I'm a winner." While I think we all understand what this father meant, the world too often scoffs at the idea of being a winner, becoming a son or daughter of God as defined by Paul.

We are confronted with a world that scoffs at such incredible possibilities, treating them as simple works of fiction or acts of fancy. When not directly scoffing at the doctrine, the world presents an image of the nature of man that runs contrary to God's description. Overt sexualization, emphasis on attaining worldly status or praise, mockery of the divinely inspired family structure, apathy—all these distract us and seek to pull us from obtaining the revelations described above. Even if we are aware of these distractions, we can struggle with the challenge of defining ourselves. Confronting these and other worldly viewpoints, we find ourselves like the young boy on the plane, trying to remind ourselves of our eternal nature while everything else tells us otherwise. This can be a very lonely experience, and unfortunately for many, the exhaustion of this struggle becomes too much and the Spirit's whispering that we are the children of God becomes lost as background noise.

Christ himself understands we often toil under false impressions of self-worth imposed on us by the world. His gentle admonition that we relieve ourselves of burdens speaks not of physical hardships, but the mental suppositions through which we see ourselves and the world around us, even if we do not recognize those suppositions immediately. It is at this point that Christ's supernal work and ministry becomes the foundation to the restoration of these truths. As the prophets make clear both in the scriptures and in modern discourse, the primary function of the Atonement is to cleanse us from the eternal consequences of wrongdoing so that we can return and dwell in God's presence as exalted beings ourselves. While the process of repentance is often discussed among the members of this church, and rightly so, an important part of the repentance process can be overlooked—obtaining the revelation that forgiveness has been achieved. Christ's Atonement not only cleanses us from the full consequences of sin but is the means by which the revelatory relationship between ourselves and God is restored. Indeed, without the revelation that we are clean before the Lord, the full blessings of forgiveness cannot be obtained. What we are offered through the Atonement is the opportunity to see anew, to "see afar off," as Peter suggested (2 Peter 1:9), to see truly who we are and what we are to become.

Jesus himself teaches this principle in his powerful parable of the prodigal son. According to Luke 15, the younger son of a wealthy man wasted his inheritance early on "riotous living." After coming to his senses, the young man realized his horrible situation and stated, "I will arise and go to my father, and will say unto him, Father, I have sinned against heaven, and before thee, and am no more worthy to be called thy son" (vv. 18–19). The difference between being offspring and son becomes the central point of the entire parable as the young man arrives and repeats his confession, whereupon his father provides him clothing and a signet ring as well as a fatted calf. The actions of the father show that he has not only taken the young man in but also restored him to the status of son. The significance of sonship is revealed in the Father's words to his older son: "Son, thou art ever with me, and all that I have is thine. It was meet that we should make merry, and be glad: for this thy brother was dead, and is alive again; and was lost, and is found" (vv. 31–32). As this parable suggests, in the divine perspective all may become sons and daughters, each receiving all that the Father hath. Thus the older son, who remained faithful, is promised his reward, and the younger man, who was once lost, is given the opportunity to become a son again.

CHRIST'S POWER TO TRANSFORM US

Throughout his ministry, Jesus provided the means for individuals to transform the very way they understood themselves. To a Canaanite woman, Jesus revealed her true standing before God. To a Samaritan woman, he taught about living water and gave her the opportunity to become the first witness to others. To a naked and disturbed young man, Christ restored his "right mind," literally clothing his nakedness and giving him an honored place at his feet. To Peter, he beckoned to walk on the stormy water, giving Peter the understanding that such a feat was not just possible but actually attainable. In all these instances, Christ gave the individual a new perspective, a new way of understanding who they were and their relationship to God. In the process, they found power to do things they had never before considered. So it is with repentance, which offers us a new perspective. Christ's exhortations tell us that forgiveness is achievable, that one really can become a son or daughter of God, but this can be done only by accepting the power of the Atonement in our lives. Thus repentance empowers us, revealing to us our real worth in the eyes of God and showing us that we are worthy of his atoning power and that the promised transformation is real. In other words, as we repent, we recognize our intrinsic value and know that God sees that same intrinsic value in us. This results in greater transformative power as we understand that the channels of revelation are made available to us again.

These principles are illustrated in the Book of Mormon narrative described in Alma 15 as Alma and Amulek meet again with Zeezrom. Following their deliverance from the Ammonihahite prison, the two missionary-prophets went to Sidon and met with the righteous refugees. Included in this group was Zeezrom, an individual who had challenged the teachings and authority of both missionaries earlier. According to the record, he was dying, suffering from a fever. His fever, we are told, was caused by "the great tribulations of his mind on account of his wickedness, for he supposed that Alma and Amulek were no more; and he supposed that they had been slain because of his iniquity. And this great sin, and his many other sins, did harrow up his mind until it did become exceedingly sore, having no deliverance; therefore he began to be scorched with a burning heat" (v. 3).

Though the affliction described here as "a sore mind" sounds vague, there is a surprising amount of information within the text concerning what causes his sore mind and its effects. Arising from deliberation on his sins, the sore mind results from a set of consequences that he assumed had already occurred. Fixated on his relationship to these consequences, Zeezrom creates a mental negative feedback loop. Harrowed up by the guilt of his actions, he cannot escape his suppositions of guilt. Instead he mentally relives the supposed consequences of his actions again and again. His suppositions, those mental structures that govern the way in which he understands the world around him, have such a powerful effect on his cognitive abilities that he cannot think or perceive anything except through them. Moreover, he is unable to stop from fixating on these suppositions. Like a wheel that spins in one place, there is no deliverance from these thoughts, no peace of mind. And because it is the only way in which he can view himself and the world around him and because there is no way in which to escape from them, Zeezrom is literally unable to function and live.

When Alma and Amulek arrive, Zeezrom asks them to heal him. We often associate the concept of healing with a physiological disorder, but in Zeezrom's case the physical element is merely symptomatic of what we may refer to as a thinking disorder. For the healing to be effective, it must address the root of the problem, which is his inability to escape his suppositions. Thus Alma responds to Zeezrom's plea with a question: "Believest thou in the power of Christ unto salvation?" (v. 6).

Though nothing in this query addresses Zeezrom's physical state, the question begins the healing process by suggesting that Christ can deliver him from his frenzied mind. This in turn empowers Zeezrom to make the changes necessary for his healing. Just accepting the possibility that healing can occur releases Zeezrom from the negative feedback and makes his deliverance possible.

Zeezrom answers Alma's question by stating that he does believe, whereupon Alma declares, "If thou believest in the redemption of Christ thou canst be healed" (v. 8), and almost immediately Zeezrom leaps up, his fever apparently gone and his "exceedingly sore mind" healed. As promised in John's declaration, Christ's Atonement gave Zeezrom the power to transform, not just by effecting the transformation but also by empowering Zeezrom with the knowledge that such transformation can occur. Thus the power of the Atonement not only transforms us physically but also changes the very way we perceive ourselves and the world around us. This may have been what Christ meant when he said he came "that [we] might have life . . . more abundantly" (John 10:10).

BECOMING CONFIDENT

The power that results from knowing what it means to be sons and daughters of God and that this is something that can be achieved with the power of repentance, expresses itself in a new confidence to do things that we might not have originally believed to be possible. In the book of Hebrews, ascribing this confidence to Christ as our atoning high priest, Paul wrote: "Seeing then that we have a great high priest, that is passed into the heavens, Jesus the Son of God, let us hold fast our profession. For we have not an high priest which cannot be touched with the feeling of our infirmities; but was in all points tempted like as we are, yet without sin. Let us therefore come boldly unto the throne of grace, that we may obtain mercy, and find grace to help in time of need" (Hebrews 4:14–16). Through knowledge of Christ, we gain the confidence to enter into the presence of God boldly, knowing that we belong there and that, as sons and daughters of God, we have a right to be there.

Alma implies this boldness through Christ in his famous series of introspective questions: "Have ye spiritually been born of God? Have ye received his image in your countenances? . . . Do ye exercise faith in the redemption of him who created you? . . . Do you look forward with an eye of faith, and view this mortal body raised in immortality? . . . I say unto you, can you imagine to yourselves that ye hear the voice of the Lord, saying unto you, in that day: Come unto me ye blessed, for behold, your works have been the works of righteousness upon the face of the earth?" (Alma 5:14–16). The transformation of ourselves made possible by Christ opens our imaginations to scenes of exaltation. Like Jesus, who "thought it not robbery to be equal with God" (Philippians 2:6), we too can confidently imagine being invited into God's presence. Jacob alluded to this confidence engendered by revelations made possible through Christ's Atonement when he declared, "Wherefore, beloved brethren, be reconciled unto him through the atonement of Christ, his

Only Begotten Son, . . . and be presented as the first-fruits of Christ unto God, . . . for why not speak of the atonement of Christ, and attain to a perfect knowledge of him, as to attain to the knowledge of a resurrection and the world to come?" (Jacob 4:11–12). As Jacob points out, the Atonement makes it possible to talk of exaltation not just as a lofty, abstract concept but as a real, attainable actuality. To rephrase his question, if this is so, why not speak of the Atonement's ultimate end, what it really makes possible? Why not speak confidently of gaining this most precious of gifts? Why not talk of becoming the sons and daughters of God, his heirs, sharing heirship with Christ himself? This is the purpose of the plan, and our awareness of its fulfillment, that it can be done, even that it will be done, gives us the confidence and boldness to actually accomplish it.

EXPERIENCING A MIGHTY CHANGE

Let me close with one last example. In the spring of 1991, while on my mission in West Virginia, I had the privilege of meeting and interacting with Barbara and teaching her the gospel. My companion and I were not the first missionaries that Barbara had met with; in fact, she had been introduced to the gospel years before, but she was never able to make the full transformation. She liked being around the missionaries, but for some reason she was unable to do anything more than sit at the periphery and experience the blessings of the gospel secondhand. Barbara was somewhat eccentric. She kept her house dark with heavy curtains; she rarely went outside, and when she did, she completely covered herself. Like the house, she was hidden. As for the gospel, she enjoyed discussing it, but when we challenged her to find out for herself whether the doctrines we taught necessitated a change in her life, she demurred. What this meant was she did not pray; though she participated in prayers, she never offered one. Over the weeks we met with Barbara, we got her to agree to come to church, which she did, enjoying the experience and the acceptance that was offered her by the members. She would tell us later how comfortable she felt in the meetings, though we noted that at times during the meetings she would get nervous and need to get up and walk around. She came to general conference that spring because she wanted to see what a prophet looked like, and upon doing so she received the impression that he was a prophet. According to the sister sitting next to Barbara, at some point Barbara turned to her and stated, "Now I understand." A few minutes later Barbara had to get up and walk around. We found her lying in the field next to the church obviously upset and very disoriented.

What we did not know was that Barbara suffered from dissociative identity disorder. Because of horribly traumatic experiences in her past, Barbara had found a way to shut off her whole personality, splintering it into aspects of herself. Normally these aspects remained quiescent, as long as Barbara did not experience confrontation, but the Spirit's whisperings to her at general conference challenged the adversary's own whispering campaign from years earlier. It was after this trauma that Barbara told us why she could not pray. It was not that she did not see efficacy in prayer. In fact, she loved hearing others pray. What Barbara believed was that God had no desire to hear specifically from her. Because of the horrors she had experienced earlier in her life, Barbara truly believed that she was a mistake and that God was, for lack of better term, ashamed that something like her even dwelt on his creation, thus he ignored her. Worse, Barbara believed that this was the right thing for him to do. As she told us, if she were God, she would not want something like a Barbara on her world either.

Even years later, it is hard for to me to fully comprehend how she lived a life based on this understanding of herself. Looking back, it does explain the darkened house, the dislike of public places, the difficulty in developing relationships with others, and why dissociation would occur when she felt the Holy Ghost. Unfortunately, two twenty-year-olds are not necessarily the most compassionate of individuals, but even if we were, the advice would still have been the same: "Barbara, you need to pray and find out." She needed to experience the transforming power of the Atonement and receive the revelations that the Atonement promises us concerning who we are. She needed to hear her Father reveal her worth.

Barbara agreed to be baptized as she agreed to the doctrines, but we were worried because she still had not prayed, and though the physical traumas of the past were no longer impediments to baptism, she had yet to establish a relationship with God. In light of this, I will never forget her phone call to us one particular Sunday. She called around 9:30 in the morning, and I was the lucky one who answered. At first, she was crying so hard she could not talk, but as she calmed down she told me of her wrestle with the Lord. The night before she had resolved to pray. Her decision kept her awake through most of the night, unable to rest because of her fear that God would make explicit what she had believed about herself for so many years. Finally, in the early morning hours she knelt for the first time in many years and prayed. Then she got up and walked into the bathroom. As she looked at herself in the mirror, a voice spoke to her as clear as any and said, "Barbara, you are my daughter."

That's all it took for her. This simple but profound revelation about who she really was, as opposed to who she thought she was, gave her the courage to make the rest of the transformation possible. Now, this experience was not a cure-all. Barbara still had challenges from the trauma, and her dissociative episodes still happened at times, but she had power to act now, power to become all that the promise of being a daughter of God delivers. Just as Barbara learned the true power of the first Easter that Easter season of 1991, it is my hope that this message today does the same this Easter season. May we all experience and be transformed by the revelatory power of Christ's Atonement. May we all become the sons and daughters of God.

NOTES

1. *Teachings of the Prophet Joseph Smith*, comp. Joseph Fielding Smith (Salt Lake City: Deseret Book, 1976), 288.
2. *Teachings of the Prophet Joseph Smith*, 217.

In the end, it will matter precious little what we know about a myriad of things if we have not come to know, through the power of the Holy Spirit, the God we worship.

(Paul Mann, © 1999 Intellectual Reserve, Inc. All rights reserved.)

WHAT WE WORSHIP

Robert L. Millet

IN HIS GREAT Intercessory Prayer, Jesus pleaded with the
Father to make his disciples one as they (the Father and the
Son) were one. It was earlier in that same prayer that Jesus
uttered the following timeless words: "And this is life eternal,
that they might know thee the only true God, and Jesus Christ,
whom thou hast sent" (John 17:3). This is a tremendously important message. In the end, it will matter precious little what
we know about a myriad of things if we have not come to
know, through the power of the Holy Spirit, the God we worship. This is one of the great purposes of mortality and thus
the quest of a lifetime. It is in this life that we prepare to meet
God (see Alma 34:32), that we come to know him and thereby

---

*Robert L. Millet is a professor of ancient scripture
at Brigham Young University.*

to grasp what we worship, to comprehend whom we worship (see D&C 93:19).

St. Thomas Aquinas, the great Christian philosopher and theologian, taught that in the long run we cannot really know what God is, only *what he is not*.[1] While I tend to disagree with Aquinas on this—especially in light of the above passage in John 17—it may be just as important to know what the Lord is *not* as to know what he is. In that light, let us consider some things that the Lord Jesus Christ is *not*.

1. *Jesus Christ is not a cosmic errand boy.* I mean no disrespect or irreverence in so saying, but I do intend to convey the idea that while he loves us deeply and dearly, Christ the Lord is not perched on the edge of heaven, anxiously anticipating our next wish. When we speak of God being *good* to us, we generally mean that he is *kind* to us. In the words of the inimitable C. S. Lewis, "What would really satisfy us would be a god who said of anything we happened to like doing, 'What does it matter so long as they are contented?' We want, in fact, not so much a father in heaven as a grandfather in heaven—a senile benevolence who as they say, 'liked to see young people enjoying themselves,' and whose plan for the universe was simply that it might be truly said at the end of each day, 'a good time was had by all.'"[2] You know and I know that our Lord is much, much more than that.

One writer observed:

> When we so emphasize Christ's benefits that he
> becomes nothing more than what his significance

is 'for me' we are in danger. . . . Evangelism
that says "come on, it's good for you"; discipleship that concentrates on the benefits package;
sermons that "use" Jesus as the means to a better
life or marriage or job or attitude—these all turn
Jesus into an expression of that nice god who always
meets my spiritual needs. And this is why I am
increasingly hesitant to speak of Jesus as my *personal
Lord and Savior.* As Ken Woodward put it in a 1994
essay, "Now I think we all need to be converted—
over and over again, but having a personal Savior
has always struck me as, well, elitist, like having a
personal tailor. I'm satisfied to have the same Lord
and Savior as everyone else." Jesus is not a personal
Savior who only seeks to meet my needs. He is the
risen, crucified Lord of all creation who seeks to
guide me back into the truth.[3]

How we view God is critical. As in most areas of our existence, balance is vital. On the one hand, our God is God: he is
omnipotent (all-powerful), omniscient (all-knowing), and, by
means of his Holy Spirit, omnipresent (everywhere present).
At the same time, as Enoch learned so poignantly, he is there
when we need him (see Moses 7:30). His infinity does not pre-
clude either his immediacy or his intimacy. One man stated
that "I want neither a terrorist spirituality that keeps me in a
perpetual state of fright about being in right relationship with
my heavenly Father nor a sappy spirituality that portrays God

as such a benign teddy bear that there is no aberrant behavior or desire of mine that he will not condone."[4]

2. *Jesus was not just a Galilean guru, nor was he a Samaritan Socrates.* It is indeed fascinating to read the New Testament Gospels, looking specifically for such things as what Jesus said, how he said it, how he responded to questions, and how he dealt with criticism and ridicule. To be sure, Jesus Christ was one bright man. He seemed to always have the right answer for the situation. But he was more than a teacher, more than an inspiring teacher, more than a great moral teacher. He was the Son of God, God the Son. That means he was more than a composite of intelligent answers, more than walking wisdom. In him was understanding and insight, but, more important, inside him were the powers of godliness, the powers of immortality.

I have traveled a good deal and met many persons of other faiths throughout the world, as well as many extremely bright and notable personalities who claim to have no faith at all. When the conversation turns to the person and powers of Jesus of Nazareth, too often I have heard what has become to me almost a laughable declaration: "I think Jesus was an extremely intelligent man, a great peacemaker, and a dispenser of gems of wisdom. But I do not believe he was God." There is a simple syllogism that applies to Jesus. It goes something like this: He was a great moral teacher. He claimed to be the Son of God. He was not the Son of God. Therefore he could not be a great moral teacher. Robert Stein has written:

On the lips of anyone else the claims of Jesus would appear to be evidence of gross egomania, for Jesus clearly implies that the entire world revolves around himself and that the fate of all men is dependent on their acceptance or rejection of him. . . . There seem to be only two possible ways of interpreting the totalitarian nature of the claims of Jesus. Either we must assume that Jesus was deluded and unstable with unusual illusions of grandeur or we are faced with the realization that Jesus is truly One who speaks with divine authority, who actually divided all of history into B.C.–A.D., and whose rejection or acceptance determines the fate of all men.[5]

Stripped of his divinity, his teachings concerning his own Godhood, the performance of miracles, forgiveness of sins, or his actual bodily resurrection, why would Jesus of Nazareth be so controversial? Why would people dislike such a man? Why on earth would he be crucified? I have wondered over the years how so many who read the same New Testament I do could conjure up a Jesus who is basically a simple, non-directive counselor, a sensitive ecologist who came to earth to model quiet pacifism. John Meier has written:

While I do not agree with those who turn Jesus into a violent revolutionary or political agitator, scholars who favor a revolutionary Jesus do have a point. A tweedy poetaster who spent his life spinning out parables and Japanese koans, a literary aesthete who toyed with first-century deconstructionism, or a bland Jesus who simply told people to look at the lilies of the field—such a Jesus would threaten no one, just as the university professors who create him threaten no one. The historical Jesus did threaten, disturb, and infuriate people—from interpreters of the Law through the Jerusalem priestly aristocracy to the Roman prefect who finally tried and crucified him. . . . A Jesus whose words and deeds would not alienate people, especially powerful people, is not the historical Jesus.[6]

"You can shut Him up for a fool," C. S. Lewis declared, "you can spit at Him and kill Him as a demon; or you can fall at His feet and call him Lord and God. But let us not come with any patronizing nonsense about his being a great human teacher. He has not left that open to us. He did not intend to."[7]

Jesus Christ is our Exemplar, the One identified by Joseph Smith as the prototype of all saved beings.[8] He did come to earth to show us the way, for he is the way (see John 14:6). But he is not just the model citizen. "Holding up Jesus as an example of how to live a moral life," N. T. Wright explained,

seems rather like holding up Tiger Woods as an example of how to hit a golf ball. Even if I started now and practiced for eight hours a day, it is highly unlikely that I would ever be able to do what Woods can do; and there are many people out there, younger and fitter than I, who are trying their hardest to do it and still find they can't. Similarly, watching Jesus . . . makes most of us, all but the most proud or ambitious, feel like we do when watching Tiger Woods hit a golf ball. Only more so. . . .

What's more, that we treat Jesus as a moral example can be, and in some people's thinking has been, a way of holding at arm's length the message of God's kingdom on the one hand and the meaning of his death and resurrection on the other. Making Jesus the supreme example of someone who lived a good life may be quite bracing to contemplate, but it is basically *safe*: it removes the far more dangerous challenge of supposing that God might actually be coming to transform this earth, and us within it, with the power and justice of heaven. . . . Jesus as "moral example" is a *domesticated* Jesus, a kind of religious mascot.

Further, Jesus "doesn't go about saying, 'This is how it's done; copy me.' He says, 'God's kingdom is coming; take up your cross and follow me.'"[9]

3. *Jesus is not "religious."* Let me explain what I mean. The Latin word *religio* originally referred to a binding obligation, a rather special obligation. In that sense, religion represents man's effort to apply true principles and doctrines in order to enable people to keep their obligations, their covenants with

the Almighty. You may recognize in the word *religion* the root for another word that we know quite well—the word *ligament*. A ligament is a fibrous tissue that binds or links bone to cartilage or that holds organs in place. Thus the true purpose of God-ordained religion is to link or tie mortal men and women to an immortal, glorified Deity. As the Apostle James taught, "Pure religion and undefiled before God and the Father is this, To visit the fatherless and widows in their affliction, and to keep [oneself] unspotted from the vices of the world" (Joseph Smith Translation, James 1:27). In other words, pure religion deals with two main aspects of our lives: how we treat other people, and to what extent we strive to remain free from sin in a sinful world. In this sense, God clearly is religious.

Too often, however, religion has been separated off from everyday life and simply made into another aspect or dimension of our lives. Thus we speak of our intellectual life, our athletic life, our social life, and our religious life. Religion is thus one of the pieces of the larger pie. Authentic Christianity, Brennan Manning observed, is not "a code of do's and don'ts, not a tedious moralizing, not a list of forbidding commandments, and certainly not the necessary minimum requirement for avoiding the pains of hell. Life in the Spirit is the thrill and the excitement of being loved by and falling in love with Jesus Christ."[10] True religion represents our link with God, our tie to the Infinite, and thus should and must inform and impact every other phase of our existence. In other words, religion is not something we do on Sunday, while we go about our business the other six days of the week. As Latter-day Saints, our religion is life, a 24/7 life.

One of the great challenges we Latter-day Saints face as a Church is a happy challenge—the challenge of Church growth. Not only does this mean we have to prepare more and more young people to serve full-time missions and more new converts to serve as leaders, but we must also see to it that we do not allow the Church or our personal lives to be directed solely by rules and written regulations. This is the Lord's Church, and he is at the head. Because it is his Church, it is to be conducted according to his plan and under his direction, through the Holy Spirit. If we become so sterile and fossilized in the way we do things in the Church, we may lose that marvelous spiritual spontaneity that should and must accompany the body of Christ (see Moroni 6:9; D&C 46:2). Pure religion is far less concerned with what we do than with who and what we are and what we are becoming.[11] Pure religion is a thing of the heart.

Pure religion is all about worship. Someone has observed that "what we're 'here for' is to become genuine human beings, reflecting the God in whose image we're made, and doing so in worship on the one hand and in mission, in its full and large sense, on the other; and that we do this not least by 'following Jesus.' The way this works out is that it produces, through the work of the Holy Spirit, a transformation of character. This transformation will mean that we do indeed 'keep the rules'— though not out of a sense of externally imposed 'duty,' but out of the character that has been formed within us." The writer continues by pointing out that human character "is the pattern of thinking and acting which runs right through someone, so that wherever you cut into them (as it were), you see the same person through and through. Its opposite would be superficiality: we all know people who present themselves at first glance as honest, cheerful, patient, or whatever, but when you get to know them better you come to realize that they're only 'putting it on,' and that when faced with a crisis, or simply when their guard is down, they're as dishonest, grouchy, and impatient as the next person."[12]

Archbishop William Temple is reported to have said, "It is a great mistake to think that God is chiefly interested in religion." In commenting on this statement, Barbara Brown Taylor has written, "What may matter more are the everyday ways we rise to our work, serving one another with gladness and singleness of heart, so that the life we share goes on working, not for any of us alone but for all of us together."[13]

4. *Jesus is not just my elder brother*. Latter-day Saints have insight into our eternal existence that persons of other faiths do not possess. For example, many of the things that happen to us in this life, including traumas and tragedies, are viewed with a more elevated perspective, given what we know about the fact that we lived as spirits before we were born in mortality. In our first estate, our premortal existence, we were taught, trained, and prepared to come to earth and take on a wondrous mortal body, all as a very significant part of the overall plan of salvation. John the Beloved opened his Gospel

with this statement: "In the beginning was the Word, and the Word was with God, and the Word was God. The same was in the beginning with God. All things were made by him, and without him was not any thing made that was made" (John 1:1–3). That is, in the premortal life Christ, here designated as the Word, was with our Heavenly Father. In fact, Christ was God in that first estate. As God and leader of the "noble and great ones" (Abraham 3:22; 4:1), he created "worlds without number" (Moses 1:33; 7:30; compare Hebrews 1:1–2). It is theologically appropriate, therefore, to refer to Jesus Christ as our elder brother as pertaining to the premortal life.

It is of great interest to me, however, that of the almost one hundred names given to our Lord and Savior by the Nephite prophets, the phrase "elder brother" is never used once. He is called the Almighty, the Almighty God, Alpha and Omega, Creator, Eternal Father, Eternal God, Eternal Head, Eternal Judge, Everlasting God, Father of heaven and of earth, God, God of Abraham, God of nature, Holy Messiah, Holy One of Israel, Immanuel, Keeper of the Gate, Lamb of God, Lord God Almighty, Lord God Omnipotent, Lord God of Hosts, Mighty One of Israel, Most High God, Redeemer of Israel, Supreme Being, True and Living God, and True Messiah but never "elder brother." In other words, I am convinced that because the Nephites looked upon Christ with such awe and viewed him with such majesty, it may not have seemed appropriate to them to refer to him as "elder brother"; he was God.

Elder M. Russell Ballard explained:

We occasionally hear some members refer to Jesus as our Elder Brother, which is a true concept based on our understanding of the premortal life with our Father in Heaven. But like many points of gospel doctrine, that simple truth doesn't go far enough in terms of describing the Savior's role in our present lives and His great position as a member of the Godhead. Thus, some non-LDS Christians are uncomfortable with what they perceive as a secondary role for Christ in our theology. They feel that we view Jesus as a spiritual peer. They believe that we view Christ as an implementer for God, if you will, but that we don't view Him as God to us and to all mankind, which, of course, is counter to biblical testimony about Christ's divinity. Let me help us understand, with clarity and testimony, our belief about Jesus Christ. We declare He is the King of Kings, Lord of Lords, the Creator, the Savior, the Captain of our Salvation, the Bright and Morning Star. He has taught us that He is in all things, above all things, through all things and round about all things, that He is Alpha and Omega, the Lord of the Universe, the first and the last relative to our salvation, and that His name is above every name and is in fact the only name under heaven by which we can be saved. . . .

Now we can understand why some Latter-day Saints have tended to focus on Christ's Sonship as opposed to His Godhood. As members of earthly families, we can relate to Him as a child, as a Son, and as a Brother because we know how that feels. We can personalize that relationship because we ourselves are children, sons and daughters, brothers and sisters. For some it may be more difficult to relate to Him as a God. And so in an attempt to draw closer to Christ and to cultivate warm and personal feelings toward Him, some tend to humanize Him, sometimes at the expense of acknowledging His Divinity. So let us be very clear on this point: it is true that Jesus was our Elder Brother in the premortal life, but we believe that in this life it is crucial that we become "born again" as His sons and daughters in the gospel covenant.[14]

5. *Christ is not "my buddy."* There is a natural tendency, and it is a dangerous one, to seek to bring Jesus down to our level in an effort to draw closer to him. This is a problem among people both in and outside the LDS faith. Of course we should seek with all our hearts to draw near to him. Of course we should strive to set aside all barriers that would prevent us from closer fellowship with him. And of course we should pray and labor and serve in an effort to close the gap between what we are and what we should be. But drawing close to the Lord is serious business; we nudge our way into intimacy at the peril of our souls.

There are a number of gospel ironies in the scriptures. One of them is the irony that only those who lose their lives in service to the Lord find eternal life (see Matthew 16:25–26). Jesus said on one occasion that he came not to bring peace but to bring a sword "to set a man at variance against his father and the daughter against her mother. . . . And a man's foes shall be they of his own household" (Matthew 10:34–36). How odd! Jesus is the Prince of Peace, and everyone knows that he above all would want family members to be close, to be united. He is teaching, however, that sometimes there is a cost associated with receiving and living the gospel, a price that may indeed separate you from those you love most.

Another gospel irony is that the way to get close to the Lord is not by attempting in any way to shrink the distance between us, to emphasize more of his humanity than his divinity, or to speak to him or of him in casual, colloquial language. In fact, as King Benjamin explained, you and I are enabled to retain a remission of sins from day to day by recognizing Christ's magnificence, majesty, and power and the fact that we are unprofitable servants who are less than the dust of the earth (see Mosiah 2:20–25; 4:11–12). Perhaps the greatest lesson that the mighty lawgiver Moses learned was a lesson that followed a transcendent encounter with Deity and a panoramic vision of God's creations. "And it came to pass that it was for the space of many hours before Moses did again receive his natural strength like unto man; and he said unto himself: Now, for this cause I know that man is nothing, which thing I never had supposed" (Moses 1:10).

The scriptures teach that our God is a consuming fire (see Hebrews 12:28–29). "This is no Christ the humanitarian, Christ the master of interpersonal relationships, or Christ the buddy. It is Christ the Lord and Savior who calls us to repent, change our lives, and strike out in a new direction."[15] Those who have come to know the Lord best—the prophets or covenant spokesmen—are also those who speak of him in reverent tones, who, like Isaiah, find themselves crying out, "Woe is me! for I am undone; because I am a man of unclean lips, and I dwell in the midst of a people of unclean lips: for mine eyes have seen the King, the Lord of hosts" (Isaiah 6:5). Coming into the presence of the Almighty is no light thing; we feel to respond soberly to God's command to Moses: "Put off thy shoes from off thy feet, for the place whereon thou standest is holy ground" (Exodus 3:5). Elder Bruce R. McConkie explained, "Those who truly love the Lord and who worship the Father in the name of the Son by the power of the Spirit, according to the approved patterns, maintain a reverential barrier between themselves and all the members of the Godhead."[16]

This is a terribly difficult balance to strike. We want ever so much to be close to the Lord. We seek, ever so diligently, spiritual fellowship with the Father and the Son (see 1 John 1:3). And yet we dare not presume upon the dignity and divinity of Deity.

6. *Jesus Christ is not the "god of the gaps."* Several years ago
my colleague Stephen Robinson and I were invited to spend
the day in conversation with representatives of the Southern
Baptist Convention. We talked together for about seven hours
that day, and some of the time was pleasant. At a certain point
in the conversation, however, one of our Baptist friends made
the comment, "But of course you folks do not believe in the
grace of Jesus Christ." Steve and I both leaned forward in our
chairs and proceeded to try to convince our friend that in fact
we did believe in and teach the importance of salvation by the
grace of Christ. At that point one of his associates responded,
"Yes, we understand, you believe in and worship the god of
the gaps." I replied, "I have never heard that before in my life.
Who or what is the god of the gaps?" He went on to explain
that it was his understanding that Latter-day Saints believed
in a kind of works righteousness, that men and women are
to do everything they can and expend all of their efforts and
then Jesus would fill in the remaining deficit. An hour later,
and after seeking again and again to dissuade them from their
caricature of Mormonism, we realized that we had failed.

Of course Jesus Christ, the One who makes all the difference in our salvation, will make up the difference at the time of
judgment, at least for those who have come to trust in and rely
upon him. But too often I fear that Latter-day Saints think that
men and women are expected to do their 85 or 90 percent and
leave the remainder, a small percentage, for Jesus to handle.
This is incorrect and misleading, inasmuch as it causes us to

overstate our own role in salvation and grossly understate the role of him who has bought us with his blood. The scripture that seems to lend itself to this misunderstanding, is, oddly enough, 2 Nephi 25:23: "For we labor diligently to write, to persuade our children, and also our brethren, to believe in Christ, and to be reconciled to God; for we know that it is by grace that we are saved, after all we can do."

I have met members throughout the Church who suppose that this means that Christ can only help us on the Day of Judgment when we have expended our best efforts and done everything we know how to do. First of all, who will have done everything they could have done? Who will have spent every waking hour of every day of every year serving God tirelessly and tenaciously? Only one person fits this bill, and that was the Lord Jesus Christ himself; he was the only one to live a perfectly sinless life. I sincerely believe that what Nephi is trying to teach is that we are saved by the grace of Jesus Christ—his unmerited divine favor, his unearned divine assistance, his enabling power—above and beyond all we can do, notwithstanding all we can do, in spite of all we can do. Too often we are prone to think of grace as the Lord's final boost into celestial glory hereafter. To be sure, we will need all the divine help we can get in order to qualify to go where God and angels are. But the grace of God is extended to you and me every hour of every day and is not limited to the bar of judgment.

Let me say this another way: If there had been no Atonement of Christ, no amount of good works on our part could ever, worlds without end, make up for the loss. "No matter how hard we work," Elder Ballard has pointed out, "no matter how much we obey, no matter how many good things we do in this life, it would not be enough were it not for Jesus Christ and His loving grace. On our own we cannot earn the kingdom of God—no matter what we do. Unfortunately, there are some within the Church who have become so preoccupied with performing good works that they forget that those works—as good as they may be—are hollow unless they are accompanied by a complete dependence on Christ."[17]

Similarly, Elder Dallin H. Oaks observed: "Men and women unquestionably have impressive powers and can bring to pass great things. But after all our obedience and good works, we cannot be saved from death or the effects of our individual sins without the grace extended by the atonement of Jesus Christ. . . . In other words, salvation does not come simply by keeping the commandments. . . . Man cannot earn his own salvation."[18]

Now having emphasized that one of the burdens of holy scripture, ancient and modern, is that we are saved by merit, but not our own merit; that salvation is free (see 2 Nephi 2:4); that eternal life is a gift, indeed, the greatest of all the gifts of God (see D&C 6:13; 14:7); and that there is consummate peace in trusting in and relying upon the goodness of God our Savior, I hasten to add that one of the scandals of the Christian world, a scandal into which we cannot afford to slide, is a seeming disregard for the simple statement of the Master: "If ye love me, keep my commandments" (John 14:15). In an effort not to supplement in any way the finished work of Jesus Christ, many of our Christian friends have created their own hyperorthodoxy of language and practically outlawed such words as work or labor or obedience or commandment keeping. The result is that the Christian message in the world has become less and less appealing, for the men and women who claim Christian status do not seem to live, on the whole, any differently than worldly people.[19] Their speech is impressive, but their personal lives leave much to be desired. Easy believism and cheap grace have replaced the depth of discipleship demanded by Deity.

"God loves us as we are," N. T. Wright has written,

> as he finds us, which is (more or less) messy, muddy, and singing out of tune. Even when we have tried to be good, we have often only made matters worse, adding (short-lived) pride to our other failures. And the never-ending wonder at the heart of genuine Christian living is that God has come to meet us right there, in our confusion of pride and fear, of mess and muddle and downright rebellion and sin. That's the point of the Christian gospel, the good news. . . . God's love comes to us where we are in Jesus Christ, and all we have to do is accept it. But when we accept it—when we welcome the new choir director into our ragged and out-of-tune moral singing—we find a new desire to read the music better, to understand

what it's all about, to sense the harmonies, to feel the shape of the melody, to get the breathing and voice production right . . . and, bit by bit, to sing in tune.[20]

Nephi taught that the words of the prophets are "sufficient to teach any man the right way; for the right way is to believe in Christ and deny him not; for by denying him ye also deny the prophets and the law. And now behold, I say unto you that the right way is to believe in Christ, and deny him not; and Christ is the Holy One of Israel; wherefore ye must bow down before him, and worship him with all your might, mind, and strength, and your whole soul; and if ye do this ye shall in no-wise be cast out" (2 Nephi 25:28–29).

We learn from both ancient and modern scripture of the Person and powers of Jesus the Christ: that he was God before he was born (see John 1:1–2); that through a grand condescension (see 1 Nephi 11:16–33) he left his "throne divine"[21] so as to "be like man almost"[22]; that he came into the world to be crucified and to bear the sins of the world (see D&C 76:41); that he received grace for grace and continued from grace to grace until, in the resurrection, he received a fulness of the glory and power of the Father (see D&C 93:16; compare Matthew 28:18);[23] and that as we follow our Lord's pathway, we too will receive grace for grace, we too will progress from one level of divine acceptance to a higher. We thereby tread on holy ground and emulate the sacred walk of this Prototype of all saved beings.[24] "I give unto you these sayings," the Savior declared in a modern revelation, "that you may understand

and know how to worship, and know what you worship, that you may come unto the Father in my name, and in due time receive of his fulness" (D&C 93:19).

Jesus is not only central to the plan of salvation; he is vital. We cannot save ourselves. We cannot earn our exaltation. We cannot exercise the sufficient grit and willpower to do the works of righteousness and battle against Satan on our own. Christ is our Lord, our Savior, our Redeemer, and our King. Through the medium of his Spirit, he is the Agent of the mighty change that comes to those who come unto him. He is the Lord of Hosts, the Lord of Armies, the Captain of our Salvation. He is God, and if it were not so, he could not save us. Without him, we have nothing. With him, we have everything.

NOTES

1. Thomas Aquinas, *Summa Theologiae*, Article 10.
2. C. S. Lewis, *The Problem of Pain* (New York: Touchstone, 1996), 35–36.
3. D. Stephen Long, "God Is Not Nice," in *God Is Not . . .*, ed. D. Brent Laytham (Grand Rapids, MI: Brazos Press, 2004), 49–50.
4. Brennan Manning, *Ruthless Trust* (San Francisco: Harper SanFrancisco, 2000), 107.
5. Robert Stein, *The Method and Message of Jesus' Teachings* (Philadelphia: Westminster Press, 1978), 118–19.
6. John Meier, *A Marginal Jew: Rethinking the Historical Jesus* (Garden City, New York: Doubleday, 1991), 1:177.
7. C. S. Lewis, *Mere Christianity* (New York: Touchstone, 1996), 56.
8. Joseph Smith., *Lectures on Faith* (Salt Lake City: Deseret Book, 1985), 7:9.
9. N. T. Wright, *After You Believe: Why Christian Character Matters* (New York: HarperOne, 2010), 126–27; emphasis in original.

10. Brennan Manning, *The Importance of Being Foolish: How to Think Like Jesus* (San Francisco: HarperSanFrancisco, 2005), 174.

11. See Dallin H. Oaks, "The Challenge to Become," *Ensign*, November 2000, 32–34.

12. Wright, *After You Believe*, 26–27.

13. Barbara Brown Taylor, "Working People," *Christian Century* 127, no. 6 (March 23, 2010): 35.

14. M. Russell Ballard, "Building Bridges of Understanding," *Ensign*, June 1998, 66.

15. Manning, *Importance of Being Foolish*, 51.

16. Bruce R. McConkie, "Our Relationship with the Lord," Brigham Young University devotional address, March 2, 1982; in *Doctrines of the Restoration: Sermons and Writings of Bruce R. McConkie*, ed. Mark L. McConkie (Salt Lake City: Bookcraft, 1989), 67–68.

17. Ballard, "Building Bridges of Understanding," 65.

18. Dallin H. Oaks, *With Full Purpose of Heart* (Salt Lake City: Deseret Book, 2002), 75; see also Jeffrey R. Holland, "The Atonement of Jesus Christ," *Ensign*, March 2008, 35–36.

19. See Ronald J. Sider, *The Scandal of the Evangelical Conscience: Why Are Christians Living Just Like the Rest of the World?* (Grand Rapids, MI: Baker Books, 2005); Dallas Willard, *The Great Omission: Reclaiming Jesus's Essential Teachings on Discipleship* (San Francisco: HarperSanFrancisco, 2006); Robert Jeffress, *Grace Gone Wild: Getting a Grip on God's Amazing Gift* (Colorado Springs: WaterBrook Press, 2005).

20. Wright, *After You Believe*, 62–63.

21. "I Stand All Amazed," *Hymns* (Salt Lake City: The Church of Jesus Christ of Latter-day Saints, 1985), no. 193.

22. "O God, the Eternal Father," *Hymns*, no. 175.

23. See Joseph Fielding Smith, *Doctrines of Salvation*, comp. Bruce R. McConkie (Salt Lake City: Bookcraft, 1954–56), 2:269; Bruce R. McConkie, *Mormon Doctrine*, 2nd ed. (Salt Lake City: Bookcraft, 1966), 339.

24. Smith, *Lectures on Faith*, 7:9.

TO PROCLAIM LIBERTY
TO THE CAPTIVES

Sandra Rogers

NOT LONG AFTER his final preparations for his ministry—the subjection of his mortality to forty days of fasting and his triumph over the powers of darkness in Satan's great attempt to thwart the plan of salvation by overwhelming the Son of God—Jesus of Nazareth took himself from the wilderness of Judea to his boyhood home in Nazareth. There, "as his custom was, he went into the synagogue on the sabbath day, and stood up for to read" (Luke 4:16). He was given the scrolls containing the book of Isaiah and read from the sixty-first chapter, "The Spirit of the Lord God is upon me, because the Lord hath anointed me to preach good tidings unto the meek; he hath sent me to bind up the brokenhearted, to proclaim liberty to the captives, and the opening of the prison to them that

---

*Sandra Rogers is international vice president
at Brigham Young University.*

are bound; to proclaim the acceptable year of the Lord" (Isaiah 61:1–2; see also Luke 4:18–19).

Christ taught that he was anointed to proclaim liberty to the captives. (Simon Dewey, Light and Truth. © *Simon Dewey.)*

Everyone in the room knew that this scripture referred to the eagerly anticipated Messiah. They also knew that when Jesus sat down after reading the scripture, he signaled that he was now going to give commentary on the passage he had read.[1] His next words stunned them: "This day is this scripture fulfilled in your ears" (Luke 4:21). In this brief moment in a small, inconspicuous synagogue in the dusty rural hamlet of Nazareth, Jesus calmly and succinctly announced who he was and what he had been sent by his Father to do.

In this Easter season, when I think of the scriptures that speak clearly to every heart of the mission of our Savior and the reasons why we might feel to shout "Hallelujah! He is risen!" I remember a few favorite passages.

The Lord revealed to Moses, "My Beloved Son, which was my Beloved and Chosen from the beginning, said unto me—Father, thy will be done, and the glory be thine forever" (Moses 4:2).

Isaiah foretold the great sacrifice of the Atonement, prophesying, "Surely he hath borne our griefs, and carried our sorrows: yet we did esteem him stricken, smitten of God, and afflicted. But he was wounded for our transgressions, he was bruised for our iniquities: the chastisement of our peace was upon him, and with his stripes we are healed. All we like sheep have gone astray; we have turned every one to his own way; and the Lord hath laid on him the iniquity of us all" (Isaiah 53:4–6).

Alma taught, "And he shall go forth, suffering pains and afflictions and temptations of every kind; and this that the word might be fulfilled which saith he will take upon him the pains and the sicknesses of his people. And he will take upon him death, that he may loose the bands of death which bind his people; and he will take upon him their infirmities, that his bowels may be filled with mercy, according to the flesh, that he may know according to the flesh how to succor his people according to their infirmities" (Alma 7:11–12).

Heavenly choirs of angels announced at his birth, "Glory to God in the highest, and on earth peace, good will toward men" (Luke 2:14).

Christ's invitation to all was "Come unto me, all ye that labour and are heavy laden, and I will give you rest. Take my yoke upon you, and learn of me; for I am meek and lowly in heart: and ye shall find rest unto your souls. For my yoke is easy, and my burden is light" (Matthew 11:28–30).

The Savior confirmed to the Nephites at the temple in Bountiful, "Behold, I am Jesus Christ, whom the prophets testified shall come into the world. And behold, I am the light and the life of the world; and I have drunk out of that bitter cup which the Father hath given me, and have glorified the Father in taking upon me the sins of the world, in the which I have suffered the will of the Father in all things from the beginning" (3 Nephi 11:10–11).

These verses are all eloquent testimonies of the Savior's divine purpose and ministry. I read them during the sacrament, and I especially love them at Easter. Today, however, I would like to focus on one of the phrases that Jesus read in Nazareth to announce who he was. The passage from Isaiah reads, "to proclaim liberty to the captives and the opening of the prison to them that are bound," and the quote in Luke reads, "to preach deliverance to the captives." I would like to share a few thoughts with you this Easter season on how Christ proclaims liberty, preaches deliverance to those who are captive, and opens the prisons to them that are bound.

Let me start with two questions: Who are the captives that are bound? And what is the nature of their captivity? I would like to consider with you four types of captivity. First is the captivity of physical death that comes to all as a result of the Fall of Adam (see 1 Corinthians 15:21–22; 2 Nephi 2:22–23). The second is the captivity we experience because of the actions of others or social circumstances. The third is the captivity of physical infirmities. Finally, there is the captivity we bring upon ourselves by our own choices and attitudes.

THE CAPTIVITY OF PHYSICAL DEATH

All those who live on earth will experience physical death. Mortals through the ages have attempted to stave off the captivity of death through elixirs, powders, cryonics, lotions, nutrients, and surgical procedures. Christ offers instead the promise of opening the doors of the prison to them that are bound by death. As Jacob explained, "For as death hath passed upon all men, to fulfil the merciful plan of the great Creator, there must needs be a power of resurrection. . . . Wherefore, it must needs be an infinite atonement—save it should be an infinite atonement this corruption could not put on incorruption. Wherefore, the first judgment which came upon man must needs have remained to an endless duration. And if so, this flesh must have laid down to rot and to crumble to its mother earth, to rise no more" (2 Nephi 9:6–7).

For the mortal body to rot and crumble and rise no more is a terrifying captivity in and of itself. But without the intercession of Christ, the liberator of all men and women, the end result for our spirits would have been even worse. Jacob helped us understand this end result when he taught: "O the wisdom of God, his mercy and grace! For behold, if the flesh should rise no more our spirits must become subject to that angel who fell from before the presence of the Eternal God, and became the devil to rise no more. And our spirits must have become like unto him, and we become devils, angels to a devil, to be shut out from the presence of our God, and to remain with the father of lies, in misery, like unto himself. . . . O how great the goodness of our God, who prepareth a way for our escape from the grasp of this awful monster" (2 Nephi 9:8–10).

When Christ rose from the tomb on the third day as the first resurrected being, he shattered the chains of eternal captivity for not only our bodies but our spirits as well. Perhaps it has been too easy for us all to accept this marvelous free gift as the given part of the Atonement, the part that every human being receives no matter what. And because it was given for all, we may not be nearly as appreciative of this gift as we should be. When we rejoice this Easter season because of Christ's victory over death and the great promise of resurrection and immortality, let us remember that without that resurrection, not only would our bodies have been captive to the grave, never to reunite with our spirits, but our spirits also would have been slaves to the devil, forever in misery in the clutches of the master of darkness.

When Christ took up his life again and became "the first-fruits of them that slept" (1 Corinthians 15:20), he freed all of us from the captivity of physical death and opened the door for all the other miracles of the Atonement. Through his infinite grace and our faithfulness and obedience, death is conquered and hell has no power to hold our spirits captive. Without immortality there could be no eternal life (see Moses 1:39). How grateful I am for this great gift of deliverance!

THE CAPTIVITY OF THE ACTIONS OF OTHERS

Another form of captivity from which Christ can set us free is the captivity created by others. There is no doubt that Christ has the power to free God's children from enslavement. We have the examples of the children of Israel being freed from Egyptian bondage (see Exodus 7–14); Shadrach, Meshach, and Abednego being saved from the flames of King Nebuchadnezzar's furnace (see Daniel 3: 8–28); Daniel being spared from the lions' den (see Daniel 6:10–23); Nephi being freed from the bonds inflicted upon him by Laman and Lemuel (see 1 Nephi 18:11–20); Alma and Amulek rending prison walls through their faith (see Alma 14:25–29); Lehi and Nephi, the sons of Helaman, being encircled in a pillar of fire as prison walls were destroyed (see Helaman 5:21–50); and Joseph Smith being delivered from Liberty Jail.

But we are also aware that there are many, including the most faithful of believers, who were not physically released from captivity. Convert believers and their wives and children were thrown into flames along with their holy scriptures as Alma and Amulek were forced to watch (see Alma 14:8–10), the early Christian martyrs were imprisoned and eventually crucified or cast to the lions to provide local entertainment, and Joseph and Hyrum Smith did not survive their incarceration in Carthage Jail.

How are we, then, to understand Christ's promise to preach deliverance to and liberate the captives in these circumstances? Why were not all these believers freed? Understanding the answer to the question *why* is not always easy for any of us, because such understanding is acquired only by our faith in Jesus Christ (see Philippians 4:7). That understanding necessitates, as King Benjamin taught, that we yield "to the enticing of the Holy Spirit, and [put] off the natural man and ... [become] as a child, submissive, meek, humble, patient, full of love, willing to submit to all things which the Lord seeth fit to inflict upon him, even as a child doth submit to his father" (Mosiah 3:19).

Those who can submit to the Lord's will, knowing that life is truly more than mortality and more than we know with our limited perspectives, are also able to understand that Christ can liberate the spirit even when the body is in chains. We learn from Abinadi's death by fire that God knows how his children suffer and is prepared to execute "vengeance upon those that destroy his people" (Mosiah 17:19).

Alma was constrained by the Spirit not to stretch forth his hand and save the innocent converts who were killed by the wicked Ammonihahites because "the Lord receiveth them up unto himself, in glory; and he doth suffer that . . . the people may do this thing unto them, according to the hardness of their hearts, that the judgments which he shall exercise upon them in his wrath may be just; and the blood of the innocent shall stand as a witness against them, yea, and cry mightily against them at the last day" (Alma 14:11).

Mormon noted after a terrible slaughter on both sides of a Nephite–Lamanite war that "while many thousands of others truly mourn for the loss of their kindred, yet they rejoice and exult in the hope, and even know, according to the promises of the Lord, that they are raised to dwell at the right hand of God, in a state of never-ending happiness" (Alma 28:12).

More importantly, faith and trust in Christ can turn some moments of captivity into blessings in disguise. A *Mormon Times* article tells about Alfred Young, who was twenty years old when he was taken prisoner in World War II and sent to Japan. His life was filled with "darkness, uncertainty, sickness, beatings, and starvation. One day he wanted something to read, and his friend, Jim Nelson, gave him a copy of the Book of Mormon." After his release, Alfred married, began a family, remembered Jim Nelson, and looked for Jim's church. The family was baptized and sealed in the temple. The gospel became the balm that healed the trauma of his captivity, and it ultimately saved his family. As a prisoner, Alfred had been stripped of everything humane, but when he encountered the Book of Mormon, it liberated him.[2]

In a *New Era* article, Melvin Leavitt tells the story of Piet Vlam, the second counselor in the Netherlands Mission in May of 1942. As a former naval officer in occupied Holland, he had to travel to Arnhem to register with the German officials. When he left his wife to register on May 15, he had no idea he would not see her again for three years. Along with other Dutch military officers, he was sent to Germany as a prisoner of war. Brother Vlam couldn't help but ask *why*.

One day after Brother Vlam arrived at Langwasser prison compound, a fellow prisoner began asking questions about religion. Brother Vlam knew how to answer the questions, and soon other prisoners wanted to hear about the Church. Groups were not allowed to gather, so Brother Vlam taught the gospel two men at a time as they walked around the camp. Soon the group wanted to hold worship services and found an empty barrack. A blanket covered the window so that the guards could not see them. Hymns were read, not sung, to avoid attracting the attention of the guards.

Gospel principles guided the behaviors of the prisoners in the group. The prisoners fasted despite their hunger. One received a testimony during a night of fasting and wept as he told the group the next day of the indescribable feeling of peace he had received. The men even composed an original song called "Faith."

Church activities continued until they were liberated. Seven of the prisoners were baptized. One of these prison converts became the first president of the Netherlands Stake. Through faith and trust in Christ, Brother Vlam fulfilled his calling in the mission presidency despite his incarceration.[3]

The lessons of Liberty Jail teach us that man's extremity is God opportunity.
(Liz Lemon Swindle, Joseph Smith in Liberty Jail, *courtesy of Foundation*
Arts.)

Using the example of Joseph Smith's experience in Liberty
Jail, Elder Jeffrey R. Holland shed great light on how the Savior can free those who remain bound. He said, "The lessons

of the winter of 1838–39 teach us that every experience can become a redemptive experience if we remain bonded to our Father in Heaven through it. These difficult lessons teach us that man's extremity is God's opportunity, and if we will be humble and faithful, if we will be believing and not curse God for our problems, He can turn the unfair and inhumane and debilitating prisons of our lives into temples—or at least into a circumstance that can bring comfort and revelation, divine companionship and peace."[4]

Elder Holland's "lessons from Liberty Jail" apply to all the forms of captivity that come to us because of the actions of others. Those who have suffered captivity at the hands of others—whether it is abuse of any sort, dishonesty, slander, gossip, or unfair judgment—can take comfort in the truth that Christ has the power to take those burdens from us and liberate us from the damaging effects they cause. Elder Richard G. Scott explained: "Your abuse results from another's unrighteous attack on your freedom, . . . and to compensate, the Lord has provided a way for you to overcome the destructive results of others' acts against your will. . . . You cannot erase what has been done, but you can forgive. (See D&C 64:10.) Forgiveness heals terrible, tragic wounds, for it allows the love of God to purge your heart and mind of the poison of hate. . . . It makes place for the purifying, healing, restoring love of the Lord. . . . He will heal you as you cease to fear and place your trust in him by striving to live his teachings."[5]

How does this healing occur? Elder Scott said: "The beginning of healing [and the release from captivity caused by
someone else's misuse of agency] requires childlike faith in the
unalterable fact that Father in Heaven loves you and has sup-
plied a way to heal [or liberate or deliver]. His Beloved Son,
Jesus Christ, laid down His life to provide that healing. . . . The
cure requires profound faith in Jesus Christ and in His infinite
capacity to heal."[6]

Through our faith, forgiveness, trust, and obedience, Christ
liberates us from the prisons created by the agency of others.
When we are able to understand his doctrine, rely on his love
for us, and cast our burdens upon his shoulders, looking forward with his eternal perspective, we will have regained our
freedom. By choosing him, we are delivered and bound no
more.

Additionally, we can feel we are held captive by social conditions and constraints. Bullies can intimidate and coerce us,
and they exist in far more places than the elementary school
playground. The pain and the terror of rejection or verbal and
physical abuse by others are as real as a prison cell. Too often
in today's world, youth and adults alike are intimidated—and
intimidation is a form of captivity—by those who would en-
tice, threaten, or provoke by calling evil things good and good
things evil (see Isaiah 5:20).

Each time children of God experience peer pressure to be
immoral, to feel ashamed for Christ's sake, or to respond to
any situation in an unrighteous way, their agency is being

tested by the agency of others. The myth that morality and fidelity are old-fashioned and trite can imprison more than just one individual as generations are affected by the choices perpetuated by this lie. The myth that withholding judgment or having charity means that all values are relative and should be given equal importance or loyalty creates a heavy chain that eventually traps a person in doubt and disaffection, leaving him or her to be constantly "driven with the wind and tossed" (see James 1:6). However, confidence that Christ honors those who honor him (see 1 Samuel 2:30) provides an anchor to our souls (see Ether 12:4) whereby we are capable of giving affirmative answers to those who question the "reason of the hope that is in [us]" (1 Peter 3:15). I remember one of my saddest moments as a faculty member at BYU. One of my students came to me in emotional tatters. She had come to BYU looking for a supportive community that shared her values, something she had not enjoyed being the only Mormon in her high school. Instead her peers at BYU teased, sneered at, and demeaned her because she was not willing to watch an R-rated movie. How proud I was of her! Despite the hurt of rejection "by her own," her faith carried her through the social prison created by her peers. To "stand in holy places, and be not moved" (D&C 87:8) in today's world requires faith, courage, poise, and patience.

Another potential social prison is that created by poverty and the subjugation of the poor by others. Isaiah saw the oppression of the poor as a great wickedness in his time and in the latter days (see Isaiah 3:14–15). Poverty limits options and constrains choices. The Lord knows all about poverty. He has revealed principles and strategies to break the chains of poverty. The Lord taught the early Saints of this dispensation in parable about their obligations to the poor: "And again I say unto you, let every man esteem his brother as himself. For what man among you having twelve sons, and is no respecter of them, and they serve him obediently, and he saith unto the one: Be thou clothed in robes and sit thou here; and to the other: Be thou clothed in rags and sit thou there—and looketh upon his sons and saith I am just? Behold, this I have given unto you as a parable, and it is even as I am. I say unto you, be one: and if ye are not one ye are not mine" (D&C 38:25–27).

In a revelation clarifying the principle of consecration, the Lord said,

> For it is expedient that I, the Lord, should make every man accountable, as a steward over earthly blessings, which I have made and prepared for my creatures.
>
> I, the Lord, stretched out the heavens, and built the earth, my very handiwork; and all things therein are mine.
>
> And it is my purpose to provide for my saints, for all things are mine.
>
> But it must needs be done in mine own way; and behold this is the way that I, the Lord, have decreed to provide for my saints, that the poor shall be exalted, in that the rich are made low.

> For the earth is full, and there is enough and to
> spare; yea, I prepared all things, and have given unto
> the children of men to be agents unto themselves.
>
> Therefore, if any man shall take of the abundance
> which I have made, and impart not his portion,
> according to the law of my gospel, unto the poor
> and the needy, he shall, with the wicked, lift up his
> eyes in hell, being in torment. (D&C 104:13–18)

One sister in the Philippines saved money, according to the principles of personal preparedness, to repair her home if it was struck by a typhoon. This last year, as a devastating typhoon moved toward the Philippines, she prayed that her humble home would be spared. Part of her faithful prayer was the promise that if her home was spared, she would donate what she had saved to repair her own home to others whose homes had been damaged. Her home was spared, and her money was donated to help those members who had suffered in the typhoon. Meanwhile, just a few months later, her daughter found a job that would pay her more and also give her more time to be at home with her family and to attend the temple regularly. This family is being delivered from the chains of poverty by their faith in Christ and their obedience to his precepts.

The Lord also taught an additional important principle regarding the poor:

Wo unto you rich men, that will not give your substance to the poor, for your riches will canker your souls; . . .

Wo unto you poor men, whose hearts are not broken, whose spirits are not contrite, and whose bellies are not satisfied, and whose hands are not stayed from laying hold upon other men's goods, whose eyes are full of greediness, and who will not labor with your own hands!

But blessed are the poor who are pure in heart, whose hearts are broken, and whose spirits are contrite, for they shall see the kingdom of God coming in power and great glory unto their deliverance; for the fatness of the earth will be theirs. (D&C 56:16–18)

I have a good friend from Ghana. Once she told me that the Saints in Ghana had to rely on this blessing in faith because life was so hard for the poor in Ghana. She also said that they knew their poverty would only be relieved at the Second Coming of the Savior. She said she prayed for the Second Coming constantly but feared that her prayers were "too small" to counter the "big" prayers of all of us in America who have so much and are worried about losing it.

Those who have are to avoid the snares of selfishness and greed and share what they have in order to relieve their brothers and sisters of the captivity of poverty. Those who do not have are to keep faith in the Lord's promises and avoid the

captivity of covetousness and greed. Each can do that by following the Savior.

The Lord has revealed the law of consecration, the law of
the fast, the welfare program, the principles of personal and
family preparedness, the Perpetual Education Fund, and Employment Resource Services to help break down the walls of
the prison of poverty for faithful members of the Church. Still,
the theme that continues to be repeated is that faith and trust
in the Lord break the figurative bonds of poverty. And after
observing the power of faith in the lives of many of the poor-
est in the Church, I see great spiritual blessings in their lives
because of their obedience.

For those individuals or their loved ones afflicted by social conditions and challenges, the captivity of the body or the
mind to those conditions is not unlike Joseph Smith's circumstance in Liberty Jail. Elder Holland's insight that these can,
through faith in Christ and trust in him, become redemptive
experiences provides us with the reassurance that Christ is
still and always delivering the captive, no matter the type of
prison in which that captive is bound.

THE CAPTIVITY OF PHYSICAL AFFLICTIONS

Another form of imprisonment common to our sojourn in
mortality is disease or disability. Christ's ministry was filled
with acts that delivered sufferers from pain, sickness, and in-
firmity. Over and over again, he healed all manner of sickness
and disease. Whether a person had "divers diseases and tor-
ments" (Matthew 4:24), leprosy (see Matthew 8:3), palsy (see

Matthew 8:5–13), possession by devils (see Matthew 8:16), an issue of blood (see Matthew 9:20–22), blindness (see Matthew 9:27–19), a withered limb (see Matthew 12:10–13), or was blind, dumb, lame, or maimed (see Matthew 15:30–31), Christ freed the person from those conditions. I have only named a few healings from the book of Matthew. In a review of all four Gospels, I counted more than one hundred references to Christ's healing power.

Yet just as not all those imprisoned inside walls and fences gain complete physical freedom, those imprisoned by the frailties of the body—whether caused by genetics, accident, poor care, or poor judgment on our part—may not always gain complete freedom of a healthy body or mind. Elder Dallin H. Oaks recently taught that healing the sick can come by medical science, by the prayers of faith, and by priesthood blessings. He reiterated that God "manifesteth himself unto all those who believe in him, by the power of the Holy Ghost; yea, unto every nation, kindred, tongue, and people, working mighty miracles . . . among the children of men according to their faith" (2 Nephi 26:13). But Elder Oaks also noted, "Faith and the healing power of the priesthood cannot produce a result contrary to the will of Him whose priesthood it is. . . . The Lord's promise is that 'he that hath faith in me to be healed, *and is not appointed unto death*, shall be healed' (D&C 42:48; emphasis added)."[7] Elder Oaks then illustrated the faith and trust involved in presenting all our various pains to the Lord. He said, "As children of God, knowing of His great love and His ultimate knowledge of what is best for our eternal welfare, we trust in Him. . . . I felt that . . . trust in the words of the father of [a] choice girl whose life was taken by cancer in her teen years. He declared, 'Our family's faith is in Jesus Christ and is not dependent on outcomes.' . . . We do all that we can for the healing of a loved one, and then we trust in the Lord for the outcome."[8]

Elder Merrill J. Bateman once told the story of a young girl who suffered from a rare disease called glutaric acidemia, which causes great pain and paralysis. The girl was confined to a wheelchair and could not speak, though she could send messages with her eyes. A gifted teacher was able to work patiently with the girl and learned that her favorite hymn was "There Is Sunshine in My Soul Today," particularly the verse that reads,

> There is music in my soul today.
> A carol to my King,
> And Jesus listening can hear
> The songs I cannot sing.[9]

Feeling guided by the Spirit, the teacher asked, "'Does Jesus listen? Does He hear the songs you cannot sing? . . . Does Jesus talk to you in your mind and in your heart? . . . Does Jesus say, 'Heather, I love you'? . . . Does he say, 'Heather, be patient; I have great things in store for you'?" The intensity of the girl's eyes penetrated the teacher's soul. The girl "knew she was loved. She knew she was special. She knew she only needed to be patient because great things were in store for her."[10] Christ's love and comfort provided solace to a little girl whose faith assured her that through his power she would be restored to a "proper and perfect frame" (Alma 40:23).

THE CAPTIVITY OF OUR OWN WRONG CHOICES

The last type of captivity experienced by all human beings is the captivity we create by our own agency. As the Apostle Paul said, "For all have sinned, and come short of the glory of God" (Romans 3:23). Sometimes we sin because of ignorance, sometimes because of our weaknesses, and sometimes because we decide to be willfully disobedient. Regardless of the reason, through the love of our Heavenly Father and the sacrifice of his Beloved Son, we can repent and be freed of the consequences of unrighteous choices.[11]

Throughout every age, the Lord has stretched forth his hand urging and imploring us to repent and return to him. Lehi taught that "redemption cometh in and through the Holy Messiah; for he is full of grace and truth. Behold, he offereth himself a sacrifice for sin, to answer the ends of the law, unto all those who have a broken heart and a contrite spirit; and unto none else can the ends of the law be answered" (2 Nephi 2:6–7). Jacob added this plea, "O, my beloved brethren, turn away from your sins; shake off the chains of him that would bind you fast; come unto that God who is the rock of your salvation" (2 Nephi 9:45).

True faith in Christ will propel us to action, to do all that we can do to partake of his redeeming grace offered to us through the Atonement. That faith builds within us such a trust and

confidence that we want to obey his commands and live by his
teachings. "As we place our faith in Jesus Christ, becoming His
obedient disciples, Heavenly Father will forgive our sins and
prepare us to return to Him."[12]

As one who has had to confront my own sins and continues to do so, I have taken great comfort in the words of Ezekiel: "If he turn from his sin, and do that which is lawful and
right; if the wicked restore the pledge, give again that he had
robbed, walk in the statutes of life, without committing iniquity: he shall surely live, he shall not die. None of his sins that
he hath committed shall be mentioned unto him: he hath done
that which is lawful and right; he shall surely live" (Ezekiel
33:14–16).

King Benjamin explained it this way:

> And again I say unto you as I have said before,
> that as ye have come to the knowledge of the glory of
> God, or if ye have known of his goodness and have
> tasted of his love, and have received a remission of
> your sins, which causeth such exceedingly great
> joy in your souls, even so I would that ye should
> remember, and always retain in remembrance,
> the greatness of God, and your own nothingness,
> and his goodness and long-suffering towards you,
> unworthy creatures, and humble yourselves even in
> the depths of humility, calling on the name of the
> Lord daily, and standing steadfastly in the faith of

that which is to come, which was spoken by the mouth of the angel.

And behold, I say unto you that if ye do this ye shall always rejoice, and be filled with the love of God, and always retain a remission of your sins; and ye shall grow in the knowledge of the glory of him that created you, or in the knowledge of that which is just and true.

And ye will not have a mind to injure one another, but to live peaceably, and to render to every man according to that which is his due. (Mosiah 4:11–13)

The hope of redemption from sin through the Atonement of Jesus Christ is the most powerful hope mankind can ever have. Think of the experience of Alma the Younger, confronted by an angel of the Lord about the seriousness of his sins and harrowed up in body and spirit by the severity of those sins. He told his son Helaman:

Oh, thought I, that I could be banished and become extinct both soul and body, that I might not be brought to stand in the presence of my God, to be judged of my deeds.

And now, for three days and for three nights was I racked, even with the pains of a damned soul.

And it came to pass that as I was thus racked with torment, while I was harrowed up by the memory of my many sins, behold, I remembered also to have heard my father prophesy unto the people concerning the coming of one Jesus Christ, a Son of God, to atone for the sins of the word.

Now, as my mind caught hold upon this thought, I cried within my heart: O Jesus, thou Son of God, have mercy on me, who am in the gall of bitterness, and am encircled about by the everlasting chains of death.

And now, behold, when I thought this, I could remember my pains no more; yea, I was harrowed up by the memory of my sins no more.

And oh, what joy, and what marvelous light I did behold; yea, my soul was filled with joy as exceeding as was my pain!

Yea, I say unto you, my son, that there could be nothing so exquisite and so bitter as were my pains. Yea, and again I say unto you, my son, that on the other hand, there can be nothing so exquisite and sweet as was my joy. (Alma 36:15–21)

Can you imagine the joyful scene in the spirit world upon the Savior's arrival after his death and Resurrection? Those who had died "firm in the hope of a glorious resurrection, through the grace of God the Father and his Only Begotten Son, Jesus Christ, . . . were filled with joy and gladness, and were rejoicing together because the day of their deliverance was at hand. . . . While this vast multitude waited and conversed, rejoicing in the hour of their deliverance from the chains of death, the Son of God appeared, declaring liberty to the captives who had been faithful" (D&C 138:14–15, 18). Those who had looked forward to this grandest of independence days, who had made the effort to repent, to improve their discipleship, to be obedient, had seen their faith rewarded.

The Savior then organized the righteous, giving them power and authority, "and commissioned them to go forth and carry the light of the gospel to them that were in darkness, even to all the spirits of men; and thus was the gospel preached to the dead. And the chosen messengers went forth to declare the acceptable day of the Lord and proclaim liberty to the captives who were bound, even unto all who would repent of their sins and receive the gospel" (D&C 138:30–31).

I also propose that we would sell the Atonement far too short if we only believe that it made it possible for us to be delivered from the burden, terrible as it might be, of our sins and transgressions. The Atonement of Jesus Christ, if we rely on it with active faith, also covers our dumb mistakes, our uninformed judgments, and our childish responses. Because of the Atonement, we are not only delivered from sin through his grace and our renewed and retuned discipleship but also given the great and magnificent opportunity to learn from our mistakes. We are not held captive by our inexperience, ignorance, and immaturity. We can actually learn and be taught. Weaknesses can become strengths (see Ether 12:27). Debts can be paid, relationships saved, wrongs righted, trust regained, and wisdom increased because Christ's Atonement gives us the gifts of progress, reconciliation, development, and improvement.

Despite these reassurances, too many of us are reluctant to leave the prisons we have built for ourselves. The Savior is knocking at the door of our cells, shoving keys under the door, and too often we ignore their presence. What is it that keeps us locked up inside the walls we have built ourselves, unwilling to take advantage of the deliverance Christ offers? Is it "because of the easiness of the way" that we hesitate or refuse to follow Christ? (see Alma 37:46).

President Ezra Taft Benson revealed the root of our imprisonment in his classic address on pride:

> Most of us think of pride as self-centeredness, conceit, boastfulness, arrogance, or haughtiness. All of these are elements of the sin, but the heart, or core, is still missing. The central feature of pride is enmity—enmity toward God and enmity toward our fellowmen. *Enmity* means "hatred toward, hostility to, or a state of opposition." It is the power by which Satan wishes to reign over us. Pride is essentially competitive in nature. We pit our will against God's. When we direct our pride toward God, it is in the spirit of "my will and not thine be done." . . . The proud cannot accept the authority of God giving direction to their lives. . . . The proud wish God would agree with them. They aren't interested in changing their opinions to agree with God's. . . . The proud

[also] make every man their adversary by pitting their intellects, opinions, works, wealth, talents, or any other worldly measuring device against others . . . to elevate [themselves] and diminish [others].[13]

Pride, then, keeps us captive, imprisoned, in shackles because we, ourselves, do not want to let Christ rescue us. It is the enmity or opposition we feel toward him, toward the Savior and Redeemer of the World that prevents us from moving from exquisite pain to exquisite joy. The War in Heaven, fought between the forces of Lucifer and the forces of Christ, is raging again in the spiritual battlefields of our own lives, and pride makes a sorry general, tactician, or strategist.

President Benson taught that the antidote for pride is humility. Is it any wonder, then, that Christ's first recorded sermons in the New Testament and the Book of Mormon include the Beatitudes? And is it any wonder that the Beatitudes offer so much counsel about humility? Christ uses the term *blessed* to describe the poor in spirit who come to him, the meek, those that hunger and thirst after righteousness, the merciful, the peacemakers, and those who are persecuted for his name (see 3 Nephi 12:3–10)—all components and attributes of humility.

The great gift of deliverance, now and in the eternities, is ours through humility. Humility is the seed of faith, the harbinger of hope, the mother of repentance, and the doorway through which the Holy Ghost can come into our lives and provide inspiration, comfort, and peace. Humility is the gateway to obedience and discipleship, the window to hearkening to counsel. Humility protects us from the mists of darkness, the filthy water, and the enticements of the great and spacious building. Humility is like a spiritual GPS unit, keeping us fixed on Jesus Christ, the fruit of the tree of life (see 1 Nephi 8).

Humility is an immunization against all that would seek to draw us away from our Savior and Redeemer. It is the filter—the spiritual bouncer if you will—that throws out the lies that are pleasing to the carnal mind (see Alma 30:53). Humility is the brake on careening desires, the corrective lens on worldly myopia, and the finely tuned hearing aid that picks up every word spoken by the Lord, through his servants, and through the Holy Ghost.

The blessings of humility include forgiveness and mercy (see D&C 61:2), direction from the Lord (see D&C 112:10), strength and knowledge (see D&C 1:28), the broken heart we offer to God as evidence of our sacrifice (see Isaiah 66:2), and the reassurance that we will not need to be compelled to be humble (see Alma 32:16).

Humility and trust in Christ allow us to grant ourselves the gift of forgiving others. I have come to learn that the commandment to forgive is more a blessing to the forgiver than the one in need of forgiveness. When we can subdue anger, contention, hurt, and pride and forgive the one who engendered those feelings in us, we turn the judgment seat away from ourselves and give it back to Christ, where it ultimately belongs (see D&C 64:10–11).

My favorite scene from the Hollywood classic *Ben Hur* is not the chariot race. It is at the very end of the movie. Ben Hur has allowed his heart to be filled with anger and revenge; he wants others to suffer as he and his family had suffered. But a change of heart occurs when he witnesses the Crucifixion of Jesus. He tells his loved ones that he heard Jesus forgive those who crucified him and that his words "took the sword out of my hand." He is freed from the shackles he had created for himself because Christ offered a better choice.

On two occasions in my life, I, like Anne Shirley of Green Gables fame, felt that I was in the depths of despair. In each circumstance, I felt that I was powerless to do anything to stop the maelstrom of challenges and difficulties going on around me. In one case, I felt that I had made so many mistakes and errors that it was now impossible for me to regain the trust and confidence of those around me. Their continued suggestions for my improvement reinforced my sense of failure. In the other case, I felt that the decisions and actions of another were pinning me in a corner and causing me to do my job inadequately. In both situations, I felt defeated and helpless.

In the first instance, I remember praying for help and guidance, fighting through my embarrassment and my pride to try to find a way to recover, to make things right, to regain trust. The answer the Lord gave me was precise and simple. It was, "Study the Beatitudes, and be more of what they say." Through that learning process, I became convinced that the Beatitudes were far more than simple little phrases to learn in

Primary. I came to understand how critical and fundamental they were, at least for me. And I came to know that unless I could be willing to learn, to take counsel, to admit mistakes, to attempt to do better, I would never progress temporally or spiritually. It was not an easy lesson to learn, and there are days when I wished I didn't have to learn it over and over again, but I am convinced it was a lesson from heaven for me.

In the second instance, I was so befuddled in my little prison cell that I became despondent, so much so that it was noticeable to others. A good friend, a colleague and a mentor, came to me one day and said, "I know you are in a bad place. I know you feel painted into a corner. I don't know how to help you, but I do know that Christ can help you if you will let him." Again, the root of my angst was my pride and the anguish of feeling that I was not measuring up because someone was taking my territory. My friend's counsel was a wake-up call. It sent me back to asking, yet again, whether I was willing to learn, to admit an error, to try again, to improve because of my faith in Christ. Again, I was asked to exchange pride for humility.

Each of these circumstances taught me that not only will pride keep you from repenting of a sin, but it will also keep you from learning and growing and improving and changing. In each case, it was the Savior—his doctrine, his gospel, his atoning sacrifice—that made change possible.

I wish I could tell you that after these two experiences I never have had to relearn those lessons. But that would be a lie. I learn them week by week and month by month in my work, in my relationships with my family and friends, and in my calling to teach teenagers in Sunday School. I continue to have the profoundest gratitude for deliverance from my errors. What despair I would experience if I felt that it was impossible to learn, to improve, and to change.

President Benson taught that humility, like pride, is our choice. He encouraged us to choose to be humble by esteeming others as ourselves, by receiving counsel and chastisement, by forgiving those who have offended us, by rendering selfless service, by going on missions and preaching the word, by going to the temple more frequently, by confessing and forsaking our sins and being born of God, by loving God and submitting our will to his, and by putting him first in our lives.[14]

Sometimes we begin a course of action that is contrary to the Lord's commandments while thinking we will always have all of our degrees of freedom. A friend once likened this attitude to swimming in the river of filthy water described in Lehi's dream (see 1 Nephi 8) but feeling okay about ourselves because the iron rod was still in sight. Suddenly we find that the prison doors are shut tightly and completely. We have allowed ourselves to participate so much in the darkness that we now are nearly incapable of turning on the light. Our habits and addictions, our spending of "money for that which is of no worth" and our laboring "for that which cannot satisfy" (2 Nephi 9:51) have eroded our agency bit by bit.

Yet the first step of any recovery from those powerful habits and addictions is to catch the glimmer of light in the darkness and follow it back to a greater light. An editorial in the *Church News* explained that in the Church's inspired recovery program, one decides to "turn your will and your life over to the care of God the Eternal Father and His Son, Jesus Christ."[15]

I am a nurse by training, and as far as I know there have been no scientific studies demonstrating the mechanisms through which brazen serpents on poles exert healing powers. We know that there were many of the children of Israel who chose not to look, as they were instructed to do by Moses, and so they were not healed from the plague of snakebites (see Deuteronomy 21:8–9). Yet all those who beheld the serpent lived. Those who refused to look perished "because they did not believe that it would heal them" (see Alma 33:20).

Our pride can keep us from looking to Christ to live. For some reason we are willing to turn to tele-counselors, talk-show hosts, and New Age philosophers for counsel and affirmation, but we don't choose to turn to the one, the Holy One, who holds the keys to all the cells in our particular prison. The winds and the waves are blowing all around us, and we keep wanting to build our houses on the sand (see Matthew 7:24).

Humility—that humility based on faith and trust in the Wonderful Counselor, the Mighty God, the Everlasting Father, the Prince of Peace (see Isaiah 9:6)—unlocks the prison doors, even when we have built those prisons ourselves. When we choose humility, we are choosing Jesus Christ. When we choose Christ, we are choosing deliverance and freedom. As Jacob so beautifully expressed, "Wherefore, men are free according to the flesh; and all things are given them which are expedient unto man. And they are free to choose liberty and eternal life, through the great Mediator of all men, or to choose captivity and death, according to the captivity and power of the devil; for he seeketh that all men might be miserable like unto himself. And now, my sons, I would that ye should look to the great Mediator, and hearken unto his great commandments; and be faithful unto his words, and choose eternal life, according to the will of his Holy Spirit" (2 Nephi 2:27–28).

My prayer is that in every season, but especially in this Easter season, we might choose liberty and eternal life through Christ, our Lord; that we also might rejoice in the liberty and freedom given to us by the Savior through his great Atonement, his suffering for us, and his triumph over death and hell. I love and worship him for giving us hope for freedom from sin and from error. I honor him for preaching deliverance to the captives and setting at liberty them that are bruised (see Luke 4:18). I praise him for opening the prison doors to them that are bound.

I testify that he lives. I know that he has done what he covenanted to do. I witness that he has and will set the captive free. I give all glory to his holy name.

NOTES

1. James E. Talmage, *Jesus the Christ* (Salt Lake City: The Church of Jesus Christ of Latter-day Saints, 1981), 179.
2. Hikari Loftus, "Book Tells Story of Captivity," *Mormon Times*, September 23, 2010.

3. Melvin Leavitt, "Missionary Focus: Captive Missionary," *New Era*, April 1977, 18–19.
4. Jeffery R. Holland, "Lessons from Liberty Jail," *Ensign*, September 2009, 28.
5. Richard G. Scott, "Healing the Tragic Scars of Abuse," *Ensign*, May 1992, 31, 33.
6. Richard G. Scott, "To Heal the Shattering Consequences of Abuse," *Ensign*, May 2008, 42.
7. Dallin H. Oaks, "Healing the Sick," *Ensign*, May 2010, 50.
8. Oaks, "Healing the Sick," 50.
9. Eliza R. Hewitt, "There Is Sunshine in My Soul Today," *Hymns* (Salt Lake City: The Church of Jesus Christ of Latter-day Saints, 1985), no. 227, verse 2.
10. Merrill J. Bateman, "The Power of Hymns," *Ensign*, July 2001, 15.
11. *Gospel Principles* (Salt Lake City: The Church of Jesus Christ of Latter-day Saints, 2009), 107.
12. *Gospel Principles*, 103.
13. Ezra Taft Benson, "Beware of Pride," *Ensign*, May 1989, 4.
14. Benson, "Beware of Pride," 7.
15. *Addiction Recovery Program: A Guide to Addiction Recovery and Healing* (Salt Lake City: The Church of Jesus Christ of Latter-day Saints, 2005), iv.

THREE STORIES

Charles Swift

E VER SINCE I was a small child, I have been in awe of stories. I am amazed by the power they have to ignite our imaginations, teach us truths, and help us feel. When I was asked to participate in this wonderful Easter Conference, I knew that I had to speak about something to do with the story of Jesus. Often when we study the scriptures, we focus on teachings that are directly conveyed by the Savior in sermons or in conversations with disciples and others. There is nothing wrong with carefully studying such passages, of course; we can learn much that is important when the Savior preaches directly to his listeners or indirectly to us readers, such as in the Sermon on the Mount. When we read "Blessed are the merciful: for they shall obtain mercy" (Matthew 5:7), we clearly understand

---

Charles Swift is an associate professor of ancient scripture at Brigham Young University.

the importance of mercy and realize that if we wish to have mercy extended to us, we need to extend it to others. However, we do not need to concentrate on the declarative in scripture at the expense of the narrative. While declarative statements in the scriptures certainly teach truth, we must remember that the stories teach truth as well. Such passages as the Sermon on the Mount are few and far between in the Gospels; most of what we are given is story. We can often learn more about mercy, for example, from experiencing a story of it in the Gospels than by reading statements about it.

The story of the Savior, as told in the Gospels, is not just any story. It is not a story created by people, though there is the element of humanity in the telling of it. It is a true story, not fabricated. But it is not just any true story. It is important to understand that it is a story with a transcendent purpose; it is not told simply for the sake of telling it. The story of Jesus is not meant to entertain or even to merely enlighten: the story of Jesus bears witness. This unique story bears witness of Jesus as the Christ, the Savior of all humanity. It is a story, a true story, *the* True Story.

I have decided to choose one chapter in one of the Gospels and take a close look at the stories there. Matthew 14 tells us three stories—two that are very well known, the feeding of the five thousand and the Savior and Peter walking on water, and one that is not as frequently discussed, in which many are healed by touching the Savior's garment. The chapter begins with an account of the Lord being told about the death of John the Baptist, but I will not discuss that account because the Savior is not the central figure.

Before I discuss these three stories, I believe it would be helpful to briefly explain what approach I am taking. First, I am staying with the King James Version of the Bible. Rather than being concerned about such issues as original authorship or the original meaning of the Greek, I am focusing on how a careful reader might understand the King James Version of these three stories without outside sources. I am looking at the text as given in the King James English, concentrating not on what the writer may or may not have intended but on what the reader can reasonably perceive. This approach is in harmony with the reader-response theory in literature with its focus on the thoughts of the reader when encountering the text.[1] That leads me to my second point: this paper is not an analysis of what scholars or other thinkers have said about these stories. Instead, I will be doing what is often called a *close reading*, in which the reader carefully explores what the text is saying by studying the text itself very closely.[2]

Discussing this approach in literary terms may seem foreign to many, but this approach shares common ground with what we often do in studying the scriptures. While we care about what the scriptures say, we also recognize that the reader can find meaning in them that may not have necessarily been intended by the original author. As Elder Dallin H. Oaks teaches, "The idea that scripture reading can lead to inspiration and revelation opens the door to the truth that a scripture is not limited to what it meant when it was written but may also include what that scripture means to a reader today. Even more, scripture reading may also lead to current revelation on whatever else the Lord wishes to communicate to the reader at that time. We do not overstate the point when we say that the scriptures can be a Urim and Thummim to assist each of us to receive personal revelation."[3]

This is a wonderful insight that can prove to be very fruitful in studying the scriptures. While we are interested in what the writer originally intended, we are not limited to that, and we must admit that we often cannot fully determine what the writer was thinking either. However, we can know what we are experiencing as we carefully study the text and respond to it. This approach does not open the door to any and all interpretations that a reader might imagine; the text needs to reasonably support the reader's understanding of it. But this approach does open the door to a much broader understanding of the scriptures that helps us to see them as living texts.

Now, let us turn our attention to the first of the three stories in Matthew 14.

FEEDING THE FIVE THOUSAND

After the disciples bury the body of John the Baptist and tell the Lord about his death, Matthew tells us that Jesus "departed thence by ship into a desert place apart" (Matthew 14:13; unless otherwise noted, all references are to Matthew 14, so hereafter only the verse will be cited). Notice how sparing the description of the action is. The writer leaves it to us to wonder what was going through the Lord's mind and heart, the grief he was experiencing. So often the mark of powerful literature is not so much what is said but what is not said. The good writer knows the power of imagination and often writes just enough to engage our thoughts and let us imagine what is happening and why it is happening. When the people hear that he has gone to a desert place, presumably to be alone and most likely to pray and commune with his Father over the death of John, "they followed him on foot out of the cities. And Jesus went forth, and saw a great multitude, and was moved with compassion toward them, and he healed their sick" (vv. 13–14). I am struck by the Savior's selflessness in this terrible situation. He has heard of his cousin's death, of the death of the prophet who prepared the way for the Lord's own ministry, of whom the Lord said, "Among them that are born of women there hath not risen a greater than John the Baptist" (Matthew 11:11). This news has apparently caused Jesus to want to be alone and contemplate what has occurred. Yet, when all these people follow him, he does not send them away, nor does he simply tolerate their presence, but he has compassion toward them and heals their sick.

Again, Matthew does not offer us the details. He does not tell us how the Lord heals the sick or how long it takes him to do so, but "when it was evening," his disciples go to him and say, "This is a desert place, and the time is now past; send the multitude away that they may go into the villages, and buy themselves victuals" (v. 15). This is quite reasonable counsel.

They are in an uninhabited place, it is late, and they do not have enough food to feed the thousands of people there, so it makes sense to send them to the villages so they can eat. There is nothing in the text to indicate that the people expect to be fed. And they have just experienced the wondrous miracle of the Lord healing their sick. Surely they can return to their homes now, content that the Lord has treated them with the greatest of kindness and generosity.

But Jesus tells the disciples, "They need not depart; give ye them to eat" (v. 16). It is easy to overlook this simple direction from the Lord. If we are not careful, we may see it as nothing more than a bit of dialogue in the middle of the story of a miracle. We may think that the purpose of the story is simply to teach us that Jesus could perform miracles by giving us an example of one. However, while Matthew leaves out details that we may think could be important, such as what exactly the Savior was going to do when he went to the "desert place," we need to approach the text as though any detail Matthew does include is important. What might this line of dialogue tell us about the Savior, beyond the fact that he did not want the people to leave but to feed them instead? How often, for example, do modern disciples of Christ, weary from a long Sabbath day of service, have yet one more person come to them in need? It may be a member of the ward, someone not of our faith, or perhaps even a spouse or a child. It may be that the Spirit will whisper to that disciple, "Do not send them away, but feed them."

Jesus tells the disciples, "They need not depart; give ye them to eat."
(Paul Mann, © 1991 Intellectual Reserve, Inc. All rights reserved.)

"We have here but five loaves, and two fishes," his disciples say. "Bring them hither to me," he responds (vv. 17–18). It is as though he is saying to you and me through this story, "Bring to me what you have. It does not matter what you have, nor does it matter how much you have. Just bring it to me. But bring it all to me, without holding anything back." I sense from this story that if the disciples had had only two loaves and one fish, it would not have mattered. I imagine the Lord would have been able to perform the miracle of feeding thousands of people if there were less than five loaves and two fishes. Likewise, if the disciples had had ten loaves and five fishes, I do not imagine he would have told them only to bring five and two. The significance is not how much the disciples had but that they were willing to give all that they had.

–"And he commanded the multitude to sit down on the grass, and took the five loaves, and the two fishes, and looking up to heaven, he blessed, and brake, and gave the loaves to his disciples, and the disciples to the multitude" (v. 19). What can we learn from the action of this story? When we bring all that we have to the Lord, he draws down the powers of heaven and blesses what we have given. He uses what we have presented to him not only to bless us but to bless others as well. I also think it is significant that he used his disciples to give the bread and fish to the thousands of people rather than doing it himself. He could have distributed the food himself, of course. But he unselfishly gave his followers the chance to receive the blessings of serving others. He teaches his disciples, the multitude, and us readers that denying someone else the blessings of service is not his way, even if a person might be able to get more done without including others. His is not a gospel of efficiency.

Another significant lesson we can learn from closely reading this text is how the Savior teaches those in the multitude who receive the food that receiving it from his servants is the same as receiving it from him. Whether the bread of life is given us directly by the Savior or by one of his servants, we are still nourished. ⸔

There is another aspect to this lesson, however. Servants are obligated to take what the Lord has given them and pass that—nothing more, nothing less—to the people. The Lord gave his disciples fish and bread to give the multitude; if they had put the fish and bread aside and given the people stones, then we cannot say that it is the same as if the Lord had given the stones to them. We must be sure that what we give others in the name of the Lord is what the Lord has given us to offer them. For example, we often quote part of a verse from the Doctrine and Covenants: "whether by mine own voice or by the voice of my servants, it is the same" (D&C 1:38). Quoting the verse in this way leaves the impression that if a person is a servant of the Lord and tells people something, it is the same as if the Lord had spoken to them, regardless of what the servant is saying. This is not the most careful of readings; we should all be servants of the Lord, but we are far from infallible, so it is not wise for anyone to think that they can take whatever we say as coming from the Lord simply because we are saying it.

It is imperative to read the entire verse: "What I the Lord have spoken, I have spoken, and I excuse not myself; and though the heavens and the earth pass away, my word shall not pass away, but shall all be fulfilled, whether by my mine own voice or by the voice of my servants, it is the same" (D&C 1:38). The full verse focuses on the *Lord's* word: "though the

heavens and the earth pass away, my word shall not pass
away, but shall all be fulfilled." If the Lord's word is being
spoken, it does not matter whether it is the Lord speaking or
his servants speaking, it is still his word. It is the same. But it
must be the Lord's word that is being spoken in order for it to
be the same. Just as the Lord gave his disciples bread and fish
and they were responsible to pass what he gave them on to the
people, so must all of us members of the Church, since we are
all his servants, be sure we receive his word from him and pass
that on to our listeners.

"And they did all eat, and were filled: and they took up of
the fragments that remained twelve baskets full. And they that
had eaten were about five thousand men, beside women and
children" (vv. 20–21). Note that everyone ate. It was not that
some ate while others remained hungry, but they all ate, and
they were all filled. If we come to him and humbly, willingly
receive what he has for us, he will not leave us wanting. No
one who comes to him will be left without. But here is an even
greater miracle: if we come to him with all that we have, we
will leave with more than we came with originally. Note that
the disciples came with five loaves of bread and two fishes but
ended up with twelve baskets full of bread and fishes. And the
multitude came with no food but were filled with food and left
with more than they came with. It is clear from the story that
some brought little and some brought nothing, but none was
turned away, and all were filled and had even more left over.
We do not have to bring the same thing to the Lord, nor do we

have to bring the same amount; we just need to try to make sure it is all we have.

WALKING ON WATER

The next story comes immediately after the miraculous feeding of those thousands of people. The Lord sends the people away and goes up a mountain by himself to pray. His disciples are on a ship that is being tossed about by the waves. Jesus comes to his disciples, walking on the sea. It is not just that this is an account of another miracle, though that is very important, but the specific act in itself is significant. The Savior is willing to enter troubled waters for his disciples. He does not stand on the shore, shouting directions or simply watching them deal with their troubles under the popular excuse that it will build their character. He comes to them.

"And when the disciples saw him walking on the sea, they were troubled, saying, It is a spirit; and they cried out for fear" (v. 26). They are disciples of Christ. They are close to him, they love him, they strive to follow him, yet they mistake who he is and what he is doing for them. He is reaching out to them, yet they are responding in fear.

"But straightway Jesus spake unto them, saying, Be of good cheer; it is I; be not afraid" (v. 27). The Lord counsels them to see him for who he is and find joy rather than fear. His coming to them, even across troubled waters and in a way they never expected, should be received with happiness and without fear.

"And Peter answered him and said, Lord, if it be thou, bid me come unto thee on the water. And he said, Come. And when

Peter was come down out of the ship, he walked on the water, to go to Jesus" (vv. 28–29). This is a fascinating piece of the story. There are at least two possible interpretations regarding Peter's comment, "Lord, if it be thou." First, he could be saying this as a kind of test—not of the Lord, necessarily, but of the still-unknown spirit that is walking on the water. The disciples are afraid, thinking that the entity on the water is a spirit or ghost. The entity claims to be the Lord, but perhaps the disciples are still not certain. Peter may be saying, in effect, "If you truly are Jesus, then you should be able to command me to walk on water and, because of your power, I would be able to do so." I do not think this interpretation requires that we readers think Peter is lacking in faith in the Lord but rather that he is not yet certain that the being on the water is who he claims to be.

A second possible interpretation is that Peter is saying, in effect, "Lord, because it is you, bid me come unto thee on the water." This interpretation assumes that Peter accepts what the person on the water has said, that he is Jesus and that Peter wants to come to his Savior but feels he cannot without the Lord giving him power to do so by bidding him to come.

Regardless of the interpretation we choose for Peter's comment, the Lord's response is clear: "Come." It is simple, concise, and direct. For me as a reader, it is also powerful, conveying a sense that the speaker can indeed make things happen by simply speaking. There is no uncertainty in that response. Jesus does not say, "Well, if you have enough faith, you can walk on water," or, "If you have sufficiently prepared yourself, you can come to me on the water," or, "If you are worthy, then it will work." Each of those responses would sow doubt in the heart of Peter. Also, each of those responses would reflect doubt in the heart of the speaker, implying that he does not know if Peter has enough faith, or is prepared, or is worthy. They are the kinds of things someone would say who does not have power and authority, who is not sure if Peter really can walk on water even if he is called to do so. As this part of the story communicates so well, Jesus is not that kind of person. When he says the simplest of words, there is sufficient power for the most miraculous events to occur.

It is also significant that Peter speaks to Jesus about bidding him to come to him and that Jesus responds by telling him to come. Peter could have said, "Lord, if it be thou, tell me I can also walk on water." And Jesus could have responded, "You can walk on water." But then the dialogue would be about whether Peter can actually walk on water. The actual words that Jesus and Peter say, however, work together metaphorically to offer an important understanding of a disciple's relationship to the Lord. Our desire should be to come unto Christ; if that is what we truly want, he will respond by inviting us to come.

There is an important phrase in this verse that is easy to overlook. When the text says that Peter is walking on the water, it includes the phrase "to go to Jesus." It seems that it is an unnecessary phrase. Peter asked the Lord to bid him to come to him, and because the Lord responded by telling him to do

The purpose of the miracle of Peter walking on the water is the same as any other miracle: "to go to Jesus." (Robert T. Barrett, © 1996 Intellectual Reserve, Inc. All rights reserved.)

so, why include this phrase? Of course Peter is going to go to Jesus—that is the sole purpose of his stepping onto the water. And that is the point: using an unnecessary phrase is a flag to the reader to ask why the phrase was used, and, in the asking, the reader discovers another important truth conveyed in this brief story. What is the purpose of this miracle of Peter walking on the water? The same purpose as any other miracle: "to go to Jesus." Whether the miracle be the healing of the sick or the raising of the dead or divine guidance in a time of adversity, ultimately the miracle is to bring us to the Lord. And, like Peter, we should not hesitate to go to the Lord right away. That should be the focus that guides our efforts.

"But when [Peter] saw the wind boisterous, he was afraid; and beginning to sink, he cried, saying, Lord, save me" (v. 30). Of course, Peter does not see the wind, but he sees the violent effects of the wind upon the water. He is actually walking on water at this point, but there are big waves and he becomes afraid. Note that he does not begin to sink and then become afraid; he fears, and then he begins to sink. Neither the winds nor the waves are sinking him: his fear is. Peter does not do what most people do when confronted with a difficult, perhaps even life-threatening problem: he does not start swimming. He does not turn to himself first, relying on his own abilities, strength, and knowledge. Instead, he immediately turns to the Lord for help—and not just for help, but to be saved. "Lord, save me" is the cry of every disciple in troubling times and one that can pertain to anything from immediate needs—physical, emotional, mental, or spiritual—to salvation and eternal life.

"And immediately Jesus stretched forth his hand, and caught him, and said unto him, O thou of little faith, wherefore didst thou doubt? And when they were come into the ship, the wind ceased" (vv. 31–32). There are several important details here worth looking at closely. Jesus did not hesitate to help Peter; he did not lecture him, try to teach him a lesson, or wait for him to take responsibility for his actions. He did not say, "If I help you, then I will have to help everyone." He just helped him, saving him from his sinking fears. And he helped him immediately. Jesus stretched forth his hand to Peter; he did not require Peter to reach up to him. It is important that the text mentions only the Lord stretching forth his hand and catching Peter.

There is one element of these last two verses that is much more than a detail, however, and lends itself to important doctrinal insights. The Lord asks Peter, "O thou of little faith, wherefore didst thou doubt?" This is the first time the word *doubt* is used in this story. Matthew does not say that when Peter saw the "wind boisterous" he doubted; he said Peter "was afraid." So which is it? Was Peter afraid or doubtful? I believe the answer lies in this basic reality of our lives: fear can lead to doubt. Peter feared the waves on the water, most likely fearing that he might drown, and this fear led to his doubting whether he could actually walk on water rather than sink. This is a fairly natural, common relationship in life. A clarinet student fears she will forget her music, so she doubts she will perform well during her recital. A young man fears that the girl he wants to ask out will refuse, so he doubts himself and decides to give up.

There is also a spiritual dimension to this relationship between fear and doubt. People can have doubts about Heavenly Father that actually have their roots in fear. And often in such cases it is helpful to ask oneself when confronted with a doubt, "What am I afraid of?" More than once, when I was a bishop of a freshman ward at BYU, a young man would tell me in an interview that he did not believe in the Book of Mormon or in Joseph Smith or even in the Savior. Of course, each young man was unique, each situation was different, and I tried my best to seek the guidance of the Holy Spirit in helping them. There were a few times, however, when there seemed to be a pattern in their thinking that led me to ask them how they would feel if the Church no longer allowed young people to serve missions. In such instances, the young man I would be interviewing would realize that he had mistaken fearing going on a mission with doubting that the restored gospel is true. Once we identified what the real issue was and he understood that he indeed had a testimony of the gospel, then we could discuss his concerns about going on a mission.

The *Lectures on Faith* teach that "those who know their weakness and liability to sin would be in constant doubt of salvation if it were not for the idea which they have of the excellency of God, that he is slow to anger and long-suffering, and of a forgiving disposition, and does forgive iniquity, transgression, and sin. An idea of these facts does away doubt, and makes faith exceedingly strong."[4] Too many of us fear that we are weak and liable to sin, so we doubt that we can be saved. But we should quit focusing on our weaknesses and instead focus on the Savior's strength. We will not be saved because we are so good; we will be saved because he is so good—so good that he performed the Atonement for our sakes. That truth does not give us license to stop keeping the commandments, but it reminds us that one of the commandments is repentance; in other words, the Lord has prepared a way for us despite our "weakness and liability to sin." If Peter had concentrated on how the Lord could give him the power to even walk on water, instead of focusing on his fear that the waves could make him sink, he would probably have been able to walk across the water and into the Savior's embrace without a problem.

"And when they were come into the ship, the wind ceased. Then they that were in the ship came and worshipped him, saying; Of a truth thou art the Son of God" (vv. 32–33). I love this closing statement of the story. The disciples on the ship worship Jesus, and, for the first time in Matthew, the disciples call him the Son of God. Matthew does not make clear why they worship him and proclaim him to be the Son of God at this particular point, however. Perhaps most readers assume they do so because they have just witnessed this amazing miracle: Jesus walking on the water. But I believe it is just as likely that they worship him and proclaim his divinity because of what they witnessed between him and Peter—the way Jesus reached out and saved him and brought him safely back to the ship. Walking on water is certainly a miracle to behold, but so is the Savior's love.

HEALING

The third story I would like to reflect on is the shortest. In fact, the other two miracles told about in this chapter are so significant and related in such relatively detailed stories that they tend to overshadow this brief account of an amazing event. After the ship arrives, Jesus and his disciples come to a land, "and when the men of that place had knowledge of him, they sent out into all that country round about, and brought unto him all that were diseased; and besought him that they might only touch the hem of his garment; and as many as touched were made perfectly whole" (vv. 35–36). It is easy for the reader to respect, even love the men of this land, so unselfish and generous as to want to be sure to bring the ill to the Lord so they could be healed. They could have gathered around Jesus to listen to his beautiful teachings as others had listened or to be miraculously fed as others had been fed, but their first concern was for the neediest among them. In fact, those needy were not even among them—the men had to seek them out. I like to picture them talking to Jesus, asking that their families and friends could simply touch the hem of his garment, as though they are careful to bother him as little as possible. The fact that all who touch his garment are healed speaks much about the power of the Savior and about the faith of those people.

This story reminds me of a story of my own from the week I was supposed to be baptized. After receiving several lessons, I told the missionaries I wanted to be baptized as soon as possible, and I met with the appropriate authority for my baptismal interview. The next day I became very ill. I was ill for the next few days, losing several pounds and not being able to keep any nourishment. I was only eighteen years old at the time, and my parents were very concerned. When they took me to the doctor, he told me that I could not be baptized that weekend, and my parents agreed. They thought I was just too ill to receive that ordinance. I was discouraged when I returned home, lying on the couch in our small living room and wondering what I could possibly do when everyone around me thought I should not be baptized. I did not want to postpone that all-important date, but I also knew that I was so ill that I had a hard time sitting up, let alone entering into a font. I was weak from not being able to eat or drink, but I could not rest knowing that I might not be able to get baptized on the following Saturday.

Then it occurred to me that there was something I might be able to do. I had heard something about priesthood blessings. I had never seen one given, I was not sure what they were, and I was not really sure who could give them or who could receive them; I just had a faint knowledge that such a thing existed. I called up my good friend who was going to baptize me on Saturday and asked if his father, a Melchizedek Priesthood holder, would be willing to give me a blessing even though I was not yet a member of the Church. I now know that not being a member of the Church would not present a problem to having a priesthood blessing, but at the time I had no idea. My friend did not know either, and he said that he would ask his father and call me back later.

I returned to the couch and prayed as I lay there. I did not know what to expect, but I felt that all my options were gone and that the only hope I had left was this thing called a priesthood blessing. I do not remember how much time passed, but the phone finally rang. It was my friend, telling me that his

father would indeed be happy to give me a priesthood blessing and asking me when he and a companion should come
over. At that moment something happened that to this day I
cannot explain. It makes no sense, especially given how badly
I wanted to receive a blessing and hopefully be healed, or at
least get sufficiently better that I could be baptized. As soon as
my friend said that I could have a blessing, I told him not to
worry about it and that I no longer needed one. He was con-
fused, of course, and asked me why I did not need one.

"I just needed to know that your father was willing to give
me a priesthood blessing," I told him. "That's enough for me.
I'll be fine now."

I hung up the phone and walked back to my couch, con-
fused myself as to why I no longer felt the need for his father
to come and give me a priesthood blessing. All I knew was that
the second I found out that the Lord's servant was willing to
come to me and bless me in his name, I sensed that the blessing, in some way I did not understand, had just been given
me by the Lord himself. Now, I have given many priesthood
blessings since and have also received many; I am certainly
not implying that priesthood blessings should not be given.
But something was different that evening in a way that I still
do not fully understand. It was as though all I had to do was
simply touch the hem of his garment, and I would be made
whole. From that moment on, I did get better, and I was able to
be baptized the following Saturday, Christmas morning.

I bear my witness that the story of the Savior is the greatest story ever told. It is a story that has power to change our lives forever, and for good. And it has that power because it is a true story.

NOTES

1. "Reader-response critics turn from the traditional conception that a text embodies an achieved set of meanings, and focus instead on the ongoing mental operations and responses of readers as their eyes follow a text on the page before them." M. H. Abrams and Geoffrey Galt Harpham, *A Glossary of Literary Terms*, 9th ed. (Boston: Wadsworth Cengage Learning, 2009), 299. Reader-response theory is a broad approach to literature with a wide spectrum of views regarding how much latitude the reader actually has.

2. Abrams and Harpham, *Glossary of Literary Terms*, 217.

3. Dallin H. Oaks, "Scripture Reading and Revelation," *Ensign*, January 1995, 8.

4. Joseph Smith, comp., *Lectures on Faith* (Salt Lake City: Deseret Book, 1985), 42.

INDEX